D0221977

Public Literacy

Elizabeth Ervin

University of North Carolina, Wilmington

 LONGMAN

An imprint of Addison Wesley Longman, Inc.

New York • Reading, Massachusetts • Menlo Park, California • Harlow, England
Don Mills, Ontario • Sydney • Mexico City • Madrid • Amsterdam

English Editor: Lynn Huddon
Supplements Editor: Donna Campion
Cover Design: Maria Ilardi Design
Text Design and Electronic Page Makeup: Dianne Hall, The Davidson Group
Electronic Project Management: David Munger, The Davidson Group

Public Literacy by Elizabeth Ervin

Copyright © 2000 Longman Publishers USA, a division of Addison Wesley Longman, Inc.

All rights reserved. No part of this publication may be reproduced, stored in a retrieval system, or transmitted, in any form or by any means, electronic, mechanical, photocopying, recording, or otherwise, without the prior written permission of the publisher. Printed in the United States.

Please visit our Website at http://longman.awl.com

ISBN: 0-321-06498-4

12345678910–DM–02010099

CONTENTS

STUDENTS' INTRODUCTION

As the writing teacher Peter Elbow once said, "School is short, life is long."[1] The purpose of this book is to assist you in doing the kind of writing you are likely to do throughout your life, beyond school and work: public writing.

Public writing can be a way of practicing good citizenship and personal initiative. It can raise awareness about important issues and establish interpersonal relationships. Although it deals with ideas, it concerns itself primarily with action—getting things done in the world.

For centuries, learning to use language for public audiences and purposes was central to all levels of schooling. Over the years, though, we have come to value other kinds of writing, and these new priorities have displaced public writing, moving it to the margins of the curriculum under the assumption that "everyone already knows how to do it." This simply isn't true. The need for thoughtful public discourse is as important now as it ever was, but for many people, learning how to engage in it requires a shift in thinking about the purposes and possibilities of writing, and new habits of paying attention.

As a means of fostering these new habits, this book introduces you to a simple but important tool that can help you to recognize and record opportunities to participate in public literacy. This tool is a writer's notebook, and we will make use of it in exercises throughout this book.[2] A writer's notebook is more than just a diary that you use to chronicle the events in your life. Rather, it's a place to collect bits and pieces of information—newspaper clippings, interesting graffiti, gossip, quotations—that may eventually lead to larger writing projects.

The point of a writer's notebook is to help you to become more curious about the world around you, and more aware of the myriad opportunities for writing that exist everywhere. Keeping a writer's notebook is a way of being ready to write at any time, and a way of never being at a loss for something to write about. Although your teacher might want to look at your writer's notebook from time to time (perhaps to read over your exercises), the notebook is primarily for your use. Therefore, you should use it to record what you think is interesting and important, even if it seems silly or insignificant at first.

What you use for your writer's notebook is completely up to you. You can purchase a cloth-bound book with an attractive cover if you like, but a spiral notebook, a sketchbook, a tablet, or just an old folder with paper in it will do just fine. The important thing isn't what your notebook looks like but how you use it. It should be convenient enough to carry around with you in a purse or book bag so that when the inspiration for writing hits or the right opportunity strikes, you'll be ready.

In this book you'll meet many people whose lives have been improved and enriched by public writing. In addition, you'll meet two college students who are new to public literacy but willing to learn more about it.

Tracy Nazarchyk is a first-generation college student from Charlotte, North Carolina. Tracy is studying English with the goal of teaching or working with community literacy programs; since her grandfather died of cancer last year, she has a special interest in hospice care, and is curious about the uses of writing among elderly and critically ill populations. Tracy is currently employed as a restaurant hostess and also has concerns about the working conditions there. Her sole experience with public literacy involved writing to a cereal company to complain about a change in her favorite breakfast food.

Pedro Marques is a student from Herndon, Virginia, a suburb of Washington, D.C. He was born in Portugal, speaks several languages, and has traveled widely, and these experiences have influenced him to major in international business and French. Pedro is very close to his immediate and extended family and is currently assisting his father in starting his own business. His main interests are traveling, reading, and sports, which he enjoys for their own sake as well as for how they might prepare him for his career. Pedro was recently elected sophomore class president at his university and used public writing to petition for candidacy and express his platform; he has also written letters of concern to various public servants.

Although you will probably be using this guide as a required textbook for school, you can make your public literacy efforts more meaningful if you see them as advancing your life goals as well as your academic goals. Margaret Mead once said, "Never doubt that a small group of thoughtful, committed citizens can change the world; indeed, it's the only thing that ever does." Public writing can be a means of changing the world for the better, one word at a time.

Notes

1. Elbow, Peter. "Reflections on Academic Discourse: How It Relates to Freshmen and Colleagues." *College English* 53 (1991): 135–55.

2. The ideas about writers' notebooks come from Randy Bomer's book *Time for Meaning: Crafting Literate Lives in Middle and High School* (Portsmouth, NH: Heinemann, 1995) and Lucy McCormick Calkins' book *The Art of Teaching Writing*, 2nd. ed. (Portsmouth, NH: Heinemann, 1994).

CHAPTER 1

What is Public Literacy?

To think about "public literacy" is to plunge into a series of questions that have preoccupied readers, writers, thinkers, and citizens for centuries: How should we define "literacy"? Who, what, and where is "the public"? What does it mean to be literate "in public," or to be a "literate member of the public"? How does "public literacy" differ from other kinds of literacy?

There are many ways to think about these questions, and this guide will not offer definitive answers. Instead, its goals are to help you to become more sophisticated about what public literacy is so that you can be more effective at writing for public audiences and public purposes. As we work toward these goals, we will use several special terms:

Public sphere refers to geographical, textual, or technological sites and forums that are accessible to people (often at no financial cost), invite their participation, and provide opportunities for that participation. Examples include sidewalks, public libraries, city council meetings, and the Internet.

Public discourse describes oral, written, and visual utterances that appear in a public sphere. Examples include community radio broadcasts, web pages, political debates, and advertising.

Public literacy designates written language, including written language that is read aloud, that appears in a public sphere and deals with issues of concern to a group of people. Bumper stickers, newspapers, tax forms, and petitions are all examples of public literacy.

Defining Public Literacy: Four Dilemmas

1. The Public and the Civic

In recent years, we've heard a lot about the supposed "deterioration" of public discourse or the "shrinking" of the public sphere. Public debate has been characterized as "the politics of personal destruction," and walls have been erected around whole communities. Critics point out that voter turnout is at an all-time low, and more and more of us are declining to get involved in everything from Boy Scouts to bowling leagues.[1]

While you might agree with this assessment, the fact of the matter is that public discourse is flourishing, thanks in part to mass media outlets like cable television and the World Wide Web. Still, it's hard to argue that tabloid newspapers and Internet pornography are just as good for democracy as neighborliness and informed public debate—which is why it's important to distinguish between *public* discourse and *civic* discourse.

Public discourse has been equated with civic discourse since the Greeks conceptualized a public sphere in the fifth century BCE. Back then, few people knew how to write, so issues were debated, legal decisions were made, and events and people were celebrated or condemned visually (through art and architecture) and orally, through music and rhetoric—a discipline which encompassed philosophy, literature, politics, oratory, and language studies. The public sphere was literally a place, or rather several places, including markets, theaters, courts, and shrines. Because all citizens were expected to participate in public debate and decision making—and because their livelihoods and status within the community often depended on their effectiveness as speakers—they often consulted teachers of rhetoric. The instructor who assigned this textbook is likely a modern version of those ancient teachers of rhetoric.

During the classical period, rhetoric was practically synonymous with public discourse. Even those texts that were written down—and that we might now enjoy privately or study in solitude, such as poetry or philosophy—were performed orally and discussed with others. Likewise, public discourse was practically synonymous with civic discourse: speech and writing that assisted in the workings of the government. In classical Greek states like Athens, sports and the arts were enjoyed as entertainment, but like law and education, they were also considered important to the development and circulation of a national culture, and thus served a civic function as well.

These attitudes continued for centuries, and were integral to the development of educational curricula. Although many of us now believe that the primary purpose of a college education is to prepare students to be successful professionals, this wasn't always the case. Until recently, college served as a "training ground" for active citizens and community leaders; rhetoric, literature, philosophy, and other disciplines were studied principally for their applications to public affairs. American universities forged connections to the public life of their communities in a variety of ways. At Harvard University in the eighteenth century, for example, this objective was formalized through such practices as "sitting solstices": oral examinations in which students' performances were evaluated not by their teachers, but by fellow citizens.[2]

Because of their long association, many people still perceive public and civic discourse to be the same thing—that is, they believe that all discourse that happens "in public" and purports to engage with "public" issues contributes to civil society. Many factors have ruptured this connection, however, including the complexity and diversity of American culture and the changing role of higher education.

2. One Public or Many?

The population of classical Athens was relatively small (fewer than 10,000 people), and "citizens" were a pretty homogeneous group: free, white, educated, middle class men. Because they shared similar cultural backgrounds, it was reasonable to assume that participants in the public sphere generally held the same beliefs and values, even if they sometimes disagreed.

This notion of a unified public sphere where everyone shares the same fundamental values has prevailed for centuries, and was a central component of eighteenth-century politics and philosophy. It was during this time that the United States formed an independent government and began to develop its own civic values, one of which was that anyone could have access to public discourse and civic life if he were smart enough, reasonable enough, and eloquent enough. Conversely, lack of reason and eloquence were the only things preventing participation in public discourse—an assumption that has been used to justify the exclusion of women, racial and ethnic minorities, immigrants, and the poor from such activities.

The turn-of-the-millennium American public is a much different setting, and yet our ideas about public discourse have been slow to change. To lament the "decline" of public discourse is to suggest that the public sphere continues to be that stable, unified place the Greeks imagined . . . but that no one is taking advantage of it. In fact, the public sphere has never really been stable and unified. The difference now is that we can no longer assume that there is a "general public" where people share the same basic values, religious beliefs, ethnic culture, or even language. Rather, we have many diverse publics. Sometimes these publics overlap or find common ground, but often they come into conflict.

Despite their diversity, publics are more than simply scattered individuals. Members of a public sphere might not know each other personally, but they are aware of themselves as part of a larger organism, and often claim a strong group identity. For example, members of the "voting public" don't know all other voters, but they're aware that there *are* other voters and that, among other things, those voters are at least 18 years old.

Even if it is no longer possible to take for granted that all Americans share the same beliefs, values, and cultural backgrounds, it is still possible for most of us to participate in and influence public discourse. Doing so, however, requires that we recognize multiple publics with diverse interests, and that we make an effort to understand the perspectives of these other publics as well as their literacy practices.

3. The Proliferation of Publishing Outlets

Plato, a fifth century BCE philosopher, believed that writing would make us lazy and forgetful, a fate which would weaken our ties to each other and, in turn, our commitment to democratic government. There might be some truth to this ancient theory (in fact, some people have made similar claims about the more recent technology of computers). But Plato also cautioned us that writing had the potential to democratize the public sphere, which we now recognize as one of the greatest *benefits* of writing.

The ability to read, write, and participate in public life hasn't always been democratic in the way we understand that concept today. In fact, these were once considered privileges reserved for the wealthy, since books, paper, and writing utensils were expensive, and few people could afford to attend school. But several phenomena have changed this situation. One is public schooling, which has made literacy education available to a wide variety of people, including non-citizens. Another is the Civil Rights movement, which has empowered non-elite members of our society to take a more active role in local and national affairs—for example, by using newspapers, political campaigns, and Websites to inform each other publicly about issues that concern them.

Because the residents of the United States are so diverse, we are interested in and concerned about a broad spectrum of issues. And because so many of us are able to read and write, we have demanded—and created—a variety of forums for reporting and debating these issues, that is, a variety of spheres in which to *publish*, or make available to a public, our ideas. Sometimes these efforts are designed to "speak to" people who already share our perspectives (as with newsletters sent to supporters of a charitable organization). Other times they are designed to reach out to other publics and encourage mutual tolerance, understanding, and cooperation (as with some letters to the editor published in newspapers).

The mass media—specifically, advertising and journalism—are important and pervasive sources of public discourse in the United States, in part because our constitution guarantees freedom of the press, and in part because we have a capitalist economy. In general, though, participation in these forms of public discourse is limited to trained professionals, not members of the lay public. This text is primarily concerned with forms of public literacy that non-professionals and non-experts can effectively participate in, and so will not emphasize journalism and advertising.

Exercise

Over the next few days, carry your writer's notebook around your campus, neighborhood, or community. Write down as many different *public spheres* as you can find: places or forums in which people publish opinions, ideas, and information. These may include newspapers, television channels, newsletters, bulletin boards, community centers, Websites, and community events; you should be able to identify many more. As you record your observations, think about how and why these public spheres differ in format, location, and the kinds of interests, concerns, or populations they represent.

4. The Public Interest

Because there are now so many places to publish our ideas, it is becoming increasingly difficult to determine who profits from public discourse. Let's take as an example a recent public service announcement (PSA) featuring comedian Bill Maher. In the PSA, sponsored by a national humane organization, Maher says, "Animal cruelty is no laughing matter."

Certainly, many people would agree that preventing animal cruelty is indeed a matter of *public interest*—of relevance or concern to everyone—whether for ethical, financial, or other reasons. But it's also possible to question whether Maher, the host of a popular television show, is doing the PSA because he is concerned about animal cruelty or because he might benefit from *publicity*—public attention—for being an animal lover.

In all fairness, Maher was a vocal supporter of animal rights long before he became famous. But the point is simply that it's not always easy to distinguish personal interest from public interest. Is an organization called "Americans for Hope, Growth, and Opportunity" really concerned with promoting economic security for all Americans, as its name suggests, or is it mainly concerned with preserving tax breaks for a small group of wealthy individuals? Do politicians really care about improving their constituents' quality of life, or are they simply seeking fame or personal gain? In other words, who benefits from public discourse?

This question is trickier than it might initially appear. Sometimes, of course, private interests are clearly at odds with public interests. For example, a few years ago a state senator, who was also a practicing lawyer, proposed a new law that was written in such a way that it would *only* benefit one of his clients, who was also one of his constituents. This represented an obvious conflict of interest.

Often, however, self interests are compatible with public interests. On a typical college campus, for instance, you are likely to see flyers selling everything from French tutoring to surfboards, and seeking everything from a roommate to a ride home. While these flyers are self-interested in that they are designed to benefit individual people, they also serve the public interest by contributing to the sense that the campus is a community whose members can appeal to each other for assistance and mutual support—financial, social, and intellectual.

Another difficulty in determining public interest is the fact that *public* is often defined as the opposite of *private*. This division is misleading. Domestic violence was regarded as a private matter in the United States until fairly recently because it usually occurred in family residences (some Americans still consider it private, as do members of many cultures throughout the world). Consequently, it was not considered appropriate or necessary to make laws or devote public resources to preventing domestic violence, punishing its perpetrators, or assisting its victims. Eventually it became clear that many of the issues that were considered private disproportionately affected women and children, many of whom spent more time at home. In the 1960s, feminists coined the phrase "the personal is political" to draw attention to the fact that things that happen "in private" often have public significance.

Exercise

In your notebook, take a few minutes to generate a list of issues that interest or concern you personally. These may include social or political causes that matter a lot to you, or simply problems or events that are on your mind. Then, in small groups, discuss ways in which your interests and concerns might have public significance. You might want to generate a list of organizations whose agendas are consistent with your interests (if you know of any), or public spheres where you could "publish" your concerns.

Once you've identified ways in which *your* interests are also *public* interests, you can begin to focus your attention on discussions of those issues, keeping an eye and ear out for opportunities to contribute to them as you read the newspaper, walk to school, talk with friends, and so on. There might be meetings, public lectures, fund-raisers, or other events or projects related to your interests that you could participate in—or, better yet, whose efforts you could assist by contributing your writing skills and rhetorical knowledge.

Tracy's list:

Will my car make it past 90,000 miles?

Why is the water evaporating out of my fish tank?

I had $150 and just paid $60 in bills.

Hurricane season starts next month.

Will my insurance cover hospital tests on Monday?

I worry if people recycle the Domino's flyers and how it is an invasion of my privacy to put them on the door because we have signs that say NO SOLICITING.

I worry about all the new buildings on campus where there used to be grass and trees (and community development too).

Pesticides on vegetables in the grocery store.

We are not very handicapper accessible at work.

Traffic: too many people run red lights and speed.

The 9–5, 2 hour parking rule downtown so people who live downtown cannot park in front of their own houses.

Not all of the items on Tracy's list have public significance—the mysterious problem with her fish tank, for example. But many of her personal concerns—such as health care, food safety, and disability rights—are issues that lots of people care about. Other issues, such as the large amount of her paycheck going toward bills, could be seen as part of broader conversations about taxes or the minimum wage.

In their small group, Pedro told Tracy about a local food co-op that sells organic produce and publishes a newsletter written by and for members. He also mentioned that the campus Environmental Concerns Organization (ECO) might share her anxieties about the environmental impact of new buildings on campus. Sometimes it can be hard for one person to make a difference in big public issues, but Pedro's suggestions illustrate how we can assist each other in finding strength in numbers.

SO WHAT?

With all this complexity and confusion over what counts as a public issue, you might be wondering why it matters whether something can be defined as public. There are several reasons, including helping you to:

- set priorities about what problems or issues are most important to you, and thus which ones to devote your energy and attention to;

- determine how decisions are made, and thus what problems or issues you can effectively influence through writing;

- identify like-minded people who might join you in building coalitions and support you in your efforts to write for public audiences and purposes; and

- discover or create opportunities to participate in public discourse at school or your workplace.

Of course, the most important decision is whether or not to participate in public discourse in the first place. As the saying goes, "If you stand for nothing you'll fall for anything." In other words, if you don't take advantage of your right to participate in public discourse, you might be taken advantage *of* by people who participate unethically. If you don't make an effort to understand and form opinions about public issues, then you're at the mercy of the people who *are* willing to make that effort.

Notes

1. Putnam, Robert D. "Bowling Alone: America's Declining Social Capital." *Journal of Democracy* 6 (1995): 65–78.

2. This example is taken from S. Michael Halloran's article, "Rhetoric in the American College Curriculum: The Decline of Public Discourse" (*PRE/TEXT* 3.3 [1982]: 245–69).

CHAPTER 2

Three Configurations of the Public Sphere

You've probably heard the terms "general public" or "average Americans" to describe people who have graduated from high school, speak English, read the newspaper, work outside the home, drive, take vacations, and so on. This description might even fit you. But what about the millions of people in this country who don't know how to read, don't have a stable job or residence, can't afford a car or a college education, and don't identify themselves as "American"? When we start to think about how many people are excluded from commonly held definitions of the "general public," it becomes clear that there's no such thing.

The myth of a general public is a remnant of the idea that there is a unified public sphere to which everyone has equal access. But as we discussed in Chapter 1, there are many public spheres, owing to a diverse population with varied public interests. And although there is considerable overlap among these public spheres—and many exceptions to the ways we might define them—it is possible to identify distinct purposes, locations, and literacy practices for each.

1. The National Public

There might not be any such thing as an "average" American, but there is something that all of us—even those who are not citizens—have in common: we are equally protected by the laws of this country, and equally responsible for obeying them. Unfortunately, there have been many situations in which laws have been applied unequally and people have received more or less than their fair share of justice, often because of their race or economic status. But it is because of these situations that public discourse continues to be important: if we perceive injustices, we have the right—some would say the responsibility—to speak out against them and enact positive changes. Writing is a tool that can assist us with such efforts.

This guide will use the term *national public* to describe the vast and diverse group of people who live in a given country, and citizens of that country who live abroad. The national public has its roots in public institutions (such as government, schools, and some mass media) and formal organizations (such as workplaces and agencies), all of which engage in different kinds of literacy activities.

In the United States, written documents that deal with laws, rights, and policies of the federal government are examples of national public literacies. Other examples include widely used public school textbooks, materials distributed by government or nonprofit agencies, national moneys, postage stamps, and some newspapers. Because not all residents of the United States speak English, and because laws, rights, and information about government services apply to everyone, these texts may appear in a variety of languages.

Of course, the United States isn't the only country with a national public sphere. All countries have them, and the public literacies of any national public inevitably reflect the values of that government. Let's take as a simple example national moneys. In the United States, all currency and coinage feature the words "*e pluribus unum*"—"from many, one"—and include likenesses of famous national monuments and, usually, former presidents; these words and images reflect this country's professed commitment to freedom and equality for a diverse citizenry, as well as its reverence for national symbols. Equally importantly, these objects represent the same amount of money for everyone—a dollar equals a dollar whether you're a stockbroker on Wall Street or a Hmong immigrant in Merced, California.

Some French money also features the national motto: "freedom, equality, brotherhood." The 50 franc note, however, rejects mottoes and monuments in favor of a portrait of the aviator and writer Alain St.-Exupéry and images of "the little prince," the title character from St.-Exupéry's famous children's story (fig. 2.1). This iconography reveals a different national culture as well as a different national monetary system.

Sometimes national public literacies amount to *propaganda*: extremely biased messages that are directed toward mass audiences in order to influence them to support special interests, especially government policies. Propaganda messages are pervasive and often

Figure 2.1. National public literacy texts like currency and postage stamps are so ubiquitous that we may take them for granted, but they can reveal much about the "official" values of a government.

show up in seemingly "neutral" settings. At the Homa Hotel in Teheran, Iran, for example, the message "Down With U.S.A." is tiled into the wall above the front door of the lobby.[1] World War II posters recruiting soldiers or appealing for civilian support are also examples of propaganda (fig. 2.2).

2. Local Publics

People often decline to participate in public literacy because "public issues" seem remote from their lives. It's true that if you read the *Christian Science Monitor* or watch the evening news, the focus is often on national or international events that seem far away, or huge issues or social problems like AIDS or health care reform that seem so abstract that it's hard to believe one person could alter their course. In reality, though, these issues often have a profound impact on our lives, and in our local communities, one person can directly influence the nature of this impact.

Figure 2.2. National public literacy documents like this 1942 propaganda poster were designed to make American civilians feel personally responsible for the outcome of World War II. The United States also published propaganda in other languages, which featured images of people of various races and ethnicities.[2]

In this book, we will use the term *local publics* to describe those people and institutions that are influenced by specific geographical locations, histories, traditions, cultures, values, and dialects. Local publics may translate national issues into specific contexts, prioritize them differently than national publics do, or ignore them altogether; they may also have unique concerns that do not affect people who live elsewhere. Local publics may be defined narrowly (e.g., as a neighborhood, borough, or city), or broadly (as a county, state, or region), and offer specific opportunities and challenges for participating in public literacy.

Examples of local public literacies include state and local laws, ordinances, or procedures; writing that promotes local events; and newspapers with primarily state, local, or regional readerships. Like national public literacies, local public literacies reflect the interests and values of a specific community. Bloomington, Illinois, for example, is like most towns in that it renounces racism. But Bloomington makes this value "official" by making racial tolerance a part of its local public discourse—specifically, by posting signs that say "Not in Our Town—No Racism" at every entrance to the city and on every municipal vehicle.

Local literacies might appear in a variety of languages and be written from highly specific cultural perspectives. For example, in neighborhoods in New York with large populations of Eastern European Jews, automatic teller machines offer instructions in Yiddish, a Hebrew dialect, as well as in English. In communities like Portland, Oregon, it is not uncommon to find a newspaper such as *These Homeless Times*, which is written entirely by the homeless and formerly homeless and oriented specifically to their experiences and concerns, but available (usually for a donation) to all interested readers.

Believe it or not, some local communities—like Ithaca, New York—actually have their own currencies. "Ithaca Hours" are locally printed and accepted along with United States dollars and cents at over 300 businesses in that community (fig. 2.3). Since Ithaca Hours represent taxable income, some people even accept them as part of their wages. Participants in the program are listed in a weekly newspaper, *Hour Town*. While citizens of Ithaca aren't required to "buy into" this alternative economic system, the fact that it exists at all, and that it is supported by many layers of local literacy texts, suggests something about the values of that community—as well as its relationship to national institutions.

Figure 2.3. Some communities print their own money depicting local landmarks, honored citizens, and slogans. These documents reinterpret national public literacies to fit local needs and priorities.

3. Everyday Publics

Not all public literacies are related to politics or solemn public issues, of course. Sometimes people use public literacy simply to have fun, share information, or build relationships. In a college dormitory, you are likely to see personal messages on doors, flyers posted in the stairwell announcing social events, and bulletin boards in the lounge documenting residents' life together. Your roommate's guacamole recipe, directions to a movie theater across town, or someone's physics notes might also be floating around. These texts can all be examples of public literacy.

Everyday publics describe people in their interpersonal relationships or informal social and political networks.[3] They may be geographically specific (e.g., invitations to a neighborhood block party), but they don't have to be (e.g., holiday newsletters that update friends and relatives about the year's events). Everyday public literacies have their roots in ordinary human experiences rather than dominant social institutions such as law, education, government, and the workplace. Because they are "unofficial" documents, they are not regulated by the formal rules, procedures, and literacy practices of these institutions, although they may be influenced by them.

Everyday public literacies tend to be quite relaxed; words might be scribbled on a napkin, with little attention to neatness or correctness, because those conventions simply aren't important to all people all the time. After a hurricane, a hand-painted sign appeared alongside the road that read "Hurican Debre" ("Hurricane Debris") and included a hurricane symbol: �??. Thanks to the sign, the workers who were collecting hurricane debris probably found the pile easily.

Often, everyday literacy texts imitate the format, language, and overall appearance of "official" literacies in order to establish credibility or authority within the local or national public sphere, as when a special interest group circulates a petition to present to the City Council. Sometimes, though, writers may adopt dominant literacy practices in order to critique national and local institutions. Consider this flyer, which was posted in the Capitol Hill neighborhood of Washington, D.C., by a residents' group who complained that police were ignoring their reports of violence and drug dealing (fig. 2.4).

At first glance, the flyer looks like a professionally designed event promotion: it includes addresses, "trademarks," and even "reviews" from the *Washington Post*. At second glance, however, it becomes clear that the flyer isn't what it appears.

Subversive forms of everyday literacy can be just as effective as national and local literacies—sometimes even more so. In this case, the flyer succeeded in summoning police to the troubled neighborhood within hours of being posted. Perhaps even more importantly, it drew national attention to the lax enforcement of national and local drug laws in our nation's capitol. (The flyer was reprinted in *Harper's* magazine.)

Figure 2.4. Everyday public literacy texts are often informal and social in orientation. This flyer, however, not only resembles a professionally designed document but also addresses a serious social issue.[4]

Exercise

Separate a page in your writer's notebook into three columns; write *national* at the top of one column, *local* at the top of another, and *everyday* at the top of the third. Then, in small groups, brainstorm examples of each kind of public literacy. Be as specific as possible. For example, instead of "billboard," write "the billboards that are supposed to be messages from God."

Pedro and Tracy's lists included the following examples:

<u>National</u>
student loan application
mailings from St. Jude's Ranch for Children (describing programs, etc.)
tax forms, tax code
Warren Commission reports

<u>Local</u>
Café Deluxe billboard "Voted favorite restaurant in the Cape Fear region!"
campaign signs for local and state candidates
university marquee—announces upcoming events on campus
schedule of events for Greek festival?

<u>Everyday</u>

note by mailboxes at apartment complex: "Apt. 1104, I got your package by mistake. Call Kristen at ——"

"Congratulations Chris and Tina—Just Married" sign propped up against a tree in someone's yard

"Just Graduated" sign in car window

"ART" spelled out in Christmas lights on roof of house downtown

Three Public Literacies in Action

Sometimes it might seem difficult to distinguish national, local, and public literacies from one another, or to see how they might influence one another. It might be useful, then, to look at an extended example.

1. National Public Literacies

The First Amendment of the United States Constitution reads:

Congress shall make no law respecting an establishment of religion, or prohibiting the free exercise thereof; or abridging the freedom of speech, or of the press; or the right of the people peaceably to assemble, and to petition the Government for a redress of grievances.

Because this document applies to—and belongs to—all Americans, it is an example of national public literacy. However, because it is also highly ambiguous, it has been interpreted in many different ways.

For example, some people believe that burning the American flag represents a legal form of political protest. Others, however, believe that this form of expression represents treason—an illegal offense—and thus support the passage of an amendment to the Constitution that explictly bans such actions. The Supreme Court and various lower courts have responded to this confusion by issuing numerous legal decisions attempting to clarify the amendment's meaning, and these decisions are likewise national public documents.

2. Local Public Literacies

Most communities require citizens to obtain permits granting them permission to assemble in public places such as parks, sidewalks, and government buildings. One form of assembly is picketing, which in Wilmington, North Carolina, is regulated by Sections 6-13 and 6-14 of the City Code. Copies of these documents, and of "Notice of

Intent to Picket" forms, are available at the local police station. The form must be filled out and approved at least a week before the scheduled event so that the police can notify the appropriate offices (e.g., Traffic Engineering) and provide necessary personnel or equipment (e.g., barricades).

Because the freedom to assemble is guaranteed by the United States Constitution, no community can prohibit public gatherings or punish those who peacefully and lawfully participate in them. However, all municipalities have the right to regulate such activities according to their local needs, traditions, and resources—as long as their policies don't violate other federal laws or rights.

3. Everyday Public Literacies

Everyday publics can sometimes publicize and assemble for events without special permission from the government, even if those events are political in orientation. For example, a neighborhood threatened by the construction of a new road posted hand-lettered signs urging people to attend an informational meeting on the subject. One such sign read:

> DON'T LET THEM RUN A HIGHWAY
> THROUGH COLLEGE ACRES!
> COME TO A PUBLIC HEARING
> MARCH 26 @ 7:00
> COLLEGE PARK ELEMENTARY
> PLEASE BE THERE!!

This sign was carefully edited, but obviously written hastily, befitting the urgency of the concern. This public hearing took place in a public building (a school) and was also announced by the newspaper. Because it was sponsored by the local government, the person or group who produced this document probably didn't have to apply for any local permits to assemble. The signs, then, represented an unofficial effort to involve neighbors in an official local event of significance to their lives.

Everyday public gatherings that take place at private residences—such as book group meetings and backyard barbecues—need no authorization from the local government. Some neighborhoods or apartment complexes may have common areas—such as clubhouses or swimming pools—with policies governing their use, but as long as these policies are adhered to, no one can prohibit such peaceful gatherings from taking place.

Exercise

As you carry around your writer's notebook, record as many different examples of public literacy as you can find. If possible, photocopy, photograph, sketch, or even take possession of the documents. (If a document is promoting an upcoming event or is someone else's property, don't take it.) Add these examples to the lists of national, local, and everyday public literacy documents you generated in small groups, and use them for ongoing consultation as you begin to make decisions about how you can participate in public literacy.

In small groups, carefully examine the documents you have found. First, decide whether they represent examples of national, local, or everyday public literacies—or some combination of these. Then, using the following questions, begin speculating about the circumstances that invited the production of each text, and make preliminary judgments about their purposes and effectiveness.

- Where was the document published (made available to a public)?
- Who wrote it?
- How was the document produced and distributed? How many copies are there? What is it written on?
- What is the document's purpose? What is it intended to accomplish?
- How might you characterize the language and tone of the document?
- What striking or unusual features, if any, do you notice about the document? What is your general impression of its quality?

Notes

1. This example appeared in Thomas L. Friedman's article "A Manifesto for the Fast World" (*New York Times Magazine* 28 March 1999: 40+).

2. Rhodes, Anthony. *Propaganda, The Art of Persuasion: World War II.* London: Angus & Robertson, 1975. 175.

3. This section is informed by David Barton and Mary Hamilton's book *Local Literacies: Reading and Writing in One Community* (London: Routledge, 1998).

4. "D. C.'s Copwatch." *Harper's* December 1998: 22.

CHAPTER 3

Finding and Creating Opportunities for Public Writing

By now you've probably got a pretty good idea about what public literacy is and why people participate in it. You might even be ready to participate in it yourself (if you haven't done so already). But participating in public literacy requires more than strong opinions and a loud voice. It also requires an understanding of when writing is the most effective of many possible actions and what it can realistically accomplish in a given situation.

Most of us can probably recall a time when we wished we'd said something publicly—spoken out against an injustice, corrected a misstatement in the newspaper, come to the defense of a friend—but didn't. Most of us can also probably recall a time when we *did* speak out but either wished we hadn't or later thought of a more appropriate response. Since "perfect" opportunities for public discourse may never present themselves, the purpose of this chapter is to help you to recognize *promising* opportunities for participating in national, local, and everyday public literacies.

Exercise

In your notebook, write about a time that you participated in public discourse (e.g., wrote a letter to the editor, attended a rally, distributed or posted flyers), or a time you thought about doing so but chose not to. Think about the reasons for your decisions and actions. What were the consequences for participating or not participating in public discourse? In retrospect, what, if anything, might you do differently?

Discuss your experiences in small groups, looking for patterns. What were common motivations for participation, or lack of it? What were some common feelings afterward? What, in general, are the "best" and "worst" circumstances in which to participate in public discourse? The "best" and "worst" possible consequences?

Rhetorical Situations

As we discussed in Chapter 1, public discourse has historically been linked to rhetoric, and a central purpose of rhetoric has traditionally been to persuade an audience to support or enact some change. Most of us could easily list a dozen things we'd like to change about the world, but not all situations invite public discourse.[1]

In order to be something other than just idle performance or self-expression, public discourse must occur within a *rhetorical situation*: a set of circumstances which calls for and can be altered by oral, written, or visual communication. This response should be a natural part of the situation, and may even be necessary for its completion. For example, the unofficial outcome of an election is typically marked by a concession speech on the part of the loser. This act of public literacy signals that the candidate has graciously accepted the defeat and wants her supporters to do likewise.

To say that a rhetorical situation "requires" language to complete it, and that this response is a "natural" part of the situation, is not to suggest that only *certain* meanings and responses are acceptable. There's nothing intrinsic about a concession speech that causes it to conclude an election; it creates that action because we agree that it does. In other words, it's simply a *convention*—a generally agreed-upon practice—that many people have come to expect and understand. Conventions aren't inflexible rules, but they can be useful as guides to what constitutes effective participation in public discourse, so it's a good idea to be aware of them.

Not all situations are rhetorical situations. In order to be "rhetorical," a situation needs to meet two criteria. First, it must be alterable: capable of being modified, corrected, improved. Second, it must be possible for this modification to be accomplished or advanced through the appropriate use of language. Imagine, for example, that you saw someone about to step in front of a car. This is a situation—a set of circumstances that requires some action or remedy. But consider which of these is the most fitting response: to yell "Hey, look out!", to go home and print up a flyer that says, "Hey, look out!", or to yank the person back onto the sidewalk?

Although this situation is alterable by several means, including appropriate use of language, it doesn't call for public literacy. But preventing *this* person from getting hit by *this* car isn't the only possible change that might be brought about by this situation. Other goals might include urging people to be more careful as they cross the street in the future, honoring citizens who do good deeds, or ensuring that busy city intersections are equipped with lighted cross-walks. All of these changes can be promoted or enacted through national, local, and everyday public literacies.

As this example illustrates, rhetorical situations usually invite many possible responses, and different responses can achieve different outcomes. Moreover, rhetorical situations can be created and shaped as well as discovered, depending on your goals and interests. (We will discuss this further in Chapter 4.) When you develop a habit of seeing the world rhetorically—as alterable through language—you are sure to notice many rhetorical situations.

When is a Rhetorical Situation Urgent?

In order to participate effectively in public discourse, it's important to recognize three components of rhetorical situations: *urgency*, *audience*, and *constraints*. While each of these features is integral to the rhetorical situation, urgency is initially the most important consideration, and so will be the focus of the remainder of this chapter.

Urgent situations are those that require immediate action or attention in order to be improved or resolved. By weighing the *urgency* of a situation, a writer can determine whether or not it is significant enough to act upon or respond to. Public discourse is an appropriate response only when urgent situations are rhetorical—that is, capable of positive modification through discourse—and when they are in the public interest (see Chapter 1).

Some situations are urgent because they are literally matters of life or death—the person stepping in front of a car, for example. It is generally considered to be in the public interest to intervene in situations that threaten the lives, health, safety, or welfare of people (and in some cases, animals and property). Other situations, however, are urgent primarily because of a person's personal commitment to an issue or problem—perhaps for moral, ethical, or financial reasons, and perhaps because their life is directly affected by it.

Consider the example of Elsie Aldrup, a senior citizen who lives in Grand Island, Nebraska. In 1974, Mrs. Aldrup's husband, Emil, died during a stay at a local hospital. Although he had expressed his desire not to be medicated, his requests were ignored and he was receiving 23 different drugs at the time of his death. Although this situation might have aroused passing resentment in some people, it bothered Mrs. Aldrup enough to sue for access to her husband's medical records, write letters to doctors and hospital administrators, distribute flyers around town, and erect signs in her yard, all in an effort to raise awareness about medical malpractice and patients' rights.

Or consider the example of Tarah Lyczewski from Sunnyside, Washington, who erected an 8-foot-tall letter "A" in her front yard after finding out that her father had moved in with another woman before his divorce from Tarah's mother was final. (The display was inspired by Nathaniel Hawthorne's novel *The Scarlet Letter*.) Certainly, Tarah's actions fall into the category of self-expression. However, they also successfully provoked vigorous local, national, and even international public debate about the issue of marital infidelity, and so can be seen as literacy that is accessible to the public and relevant to their interests.

Sometimes, even life or death situations are not considered urgent by those in a position to help. Recall the neighborhood in Washington, D.C., that was plagued by drug dealing and violence (see Chapter 2). This was an urgent situation to residents of that neighborhood, who were concerned about their safety and quality of life. However, the situation apparently wasn't urgent to local police, who ignored requests for help until publicly criticized.

The point is that situations that seem urgent to *us*—even matters of life and death—may not seem urgent to those people who could change the situations. Many of us would simply get discouraged and give up in the face of such indifference. But Elsie Aldrup, Tarah Lyczewski, and the residents of the Capitol Hill neighborhood responded by creatively transforming hopeless situations into *urgent rhetorical situations* through the strategic use of public literacy. In other words, by reimagining their problems as *alterable through public writing*, they were able to enact positive changes in their lives and worlds.

Thinking Rhetorically

You might be at the point where you start seeing opportunities for public literacy everywhere. There is an infinite supply of such opportunities, and since it's impossible to respond to all of them, you should ask yourself the following questions as you consider your options for participating in public literacy:

1. Is the situation *rhetorical?*
   - Can the situation be changed?
   - Can I imagine ways that it might be changed through writing?
   - Is writing an appropriate response to the situation?
   - Is writing likely to improve the situation in any way?

If you answer "yes" to these questions, then ask yourself:

2. Is the rhetorical situation *urgent?*
   - Does this situation affect the life, health, safety, or welfare of anyone, possibly but not necessarily including me?
     OR
   - Does the situation matter a lot to me personally?
   - Does the situation require an immediate response in order to be improved or completed?
   - Is it possible that this will be the last opportunity to use writing to improve the situation?
   - Will deferring a response make the situation worse or allow it to continue?

If you also answer "yes" to these questions, then ask yourself:

3.   Is the urgent rhetorical situation *in the public interest?*

   •   Does this issue affect many people in my country, community, or interpersonal network?
   •   Are these people aware of and concerned about the issue?
   •   Would these people benefit from the change that I wish to propose?
   •   Would they support the change I wish to propose?
   •   Would they agree that some form of public literacy is a sound course of action in this situation?

If the answers to all of these questions are "yes" or "maybe," then you have probably found a promising opportunity for engaging in public literacy and should proceed with your plans. If the answer to any of these questions is "no," then you might want to reconsider whether the situation requires a written response, a public written response, or any response at all. If the answer to any of these questions is "no" but you are committed to transforming the issue into a rhetorical situation that calls for public literacy, then you might need to rethink your goals.

Exercise

Review the interests and concerns that you have listed in your writer's notebook. If you think of new ones, add them. Then, with those interests in mind, revisit some of the public spheres you identified and see if they suggest any urgent rhetorical situations; gather or record any relevant information in your notebook. News items, press releases, and community bulletin boards are obvious places to start your search, but rumors, graffiti, and personal experiences can also offer promising leads. Finally, do some informal writing about how the issues on your list might be changed or improved—for example, how problems might be solved, how questions might be answered, or what kinds of small measures might set the stage for larger actions.

In small groups, share the results of your preliminary investigation, and work through the questions on the "Thinking Rhetorically" checklist above. If you think you have found a situation that invites public literacy, then you might want to start thinking about specific genres and audiences for your writing. We'll do this in Chapter 4.

When Pedro went back to his writer's notebook, he noticed that he had many questions and concerns about school violence, mostly inspired by various well-publicized events across the country. After he recognized this pattern in his notebook, Pedro did some informal writing and came to the conclusion that he held the news media responsible for sensationalizing the violent behavior, and he held parents responsible for not being more involved in their children's lives. Pedro was most interested in thinking about parents' roles in preventing school violence.

After completing the checklist above, Pedro was convinced that school violence represents an urgent situation that the public has an interest in addressing. For one thing, it threatens the lives and safety of many people, including students and teachers. For another, local and national newspapers routinely feature articles and letters to the editor on the subject of school violence, suggesting that it is an issue of grave concern to many citizens. Still, Pedro couldn't figure out how he might increase parental involvement in students' lives through public writing. Furthermore, he was certain that he would have future opportunities to respond to the problem—perhaps when he was more knowledgeable about possible solutions.

Pedro discussed his reservations with Tracy, who suggested that he consider ways to *improve* the problem of school violence rather than solve it—that is, take small steps to make the situation better, even if he couldn't eliminate it altogether (at least not right away). She also observed that Pedro might have a better chance of succeeding if he focused on the problem as it affected his own community. We'll examine Pedro's response to Tracy's suggestions in Chapters 4 and 6.

Tracy ran across an article in the newspaper about how a genetically altered strain of corn was shortening the life cycle of monarch butterflies, an issue that related to her concerns about pesticides in food. If you were her partner, how would you advise her to proceed?

Benefits, Risks, and Responsibilities

Writing for public audiences and purposes can be very satisfying—even when our efforts fail. People who participate in public literacy regularly report feeling more knowledgeable about the world around them, more connected to their communities, and more in control of their own lives. Successful efforts can intensify one's own commitment to public issues, inspire the participation of others, and generally make the world a better place to live.

But participating in public literacy carries risks and responsibilities, as well as benefits. Elsie Aldrup endured harassment, threats, and the destruction of her personal property for over 20 years as a result of her yard signs; moreover, she lost the support of many friends and neighbors, some of whom questioned her mental stability. Tarah Lyczewski is estranged from her father and was the subject of a public nuisance complaint when 208 of her neighbors filed a petition to have her display removed from her yard.

Although these situations represent unfortunate exceptions, taking responsibility for the opinions and claims you express publicly inevitably carries with it some risk. In most cases, though, the worst that happens is that people disagree with you, complain about you, or prove you wrong–sometimes just as publicly. Such consequences may make us think twice about voicing our concerns in a public sphere, but they represent a necessary risk: if people were not required to take responsibility for the claims they make publicly, then they might be free to make untrue or libelous statements. Facing the consequences of our words, then, can encourage us to be vigilant about forming sound opinions, reporting facts accurately, being fair to other perspectives, and creating carefully edited documents.

Note

1. The following sections are influenced by Lloyd Bitzer's article "The Rhetorical Situation" (*Philosophy and Rhetoric* 1 [1968]: 1–14) and Richard E. Vatz's article "The Myth of the Rhetorical Situation" (*Philosophy and Rhetoric* 6 [1973]: 154–61).

CHAPTER 4

Making Decisions About Content and Form

Once you have decided that a rhetorical situation is both urgent and in the public interest, you must make a number of decisions about how to proceed with your writing. Among other things, you will need to refine your goals, select an audience, and translate your ideas into an appropriate public genre. Rhetorical situations are living organisms, subject to human interpretation and manipulation as well as changing circumstances. Therefore, the decisions you make about one component of a rhetorical situation will likely affect the way you think about the whole public literacy process.

The complexity of this process can influence your efforts to participate in public literacy in positive and negative ways. On the one hand, too many decisions can be so overwhelming that they cause you to give up in frustration. But on the other hand, engaging critically with the decision-making process can assist you in imagining a range of possible responses, thus improving your chances of creating a successful public literacy document.

Choosing an Appropriate Public Genre

The content and form of public discourse are linked to *genre*: distinctive categories or types of writing, such as letters, poems, or research papers. Documents within the same genre usually share certain conventions related to form, tone, publishing strategies, and even subject matter (see Chapters 6, 7, and 8). For example, flyers usually fit on the front of one page and are generally used to announce upcoming events or offer basic information about an urgent public issue; this information often takes the form of a list rather than a narrative, and may be centered on the page. It would seem strange to see a flyer in the newspaper or on a Website. Instead, people publish this public literacy genre by passing out copies to passers-by, putting them under windshield wipers, or posting them where they are likely to be noticed by an appropriate audience.

As a general rule, genre is not the first determination you make when you participate in public literacy. In other words, you wouldn't decide to write a press release and then search for an upcoming event to write about. You would be more likely to find yourself faced with an urgent rhetorical situation and then evaluate a variety of genre options that might allow you to respond to the situation appropriately.

Exercise

In small groups, list as many different examples of public discourse genres as you can find. This book has used flyers, public service announcements, newspapers, signs, and currency as examples of public discourse genres, but you should be able to think of many, many others. As a class, generate a master list of public literacy genres. Continue to add to this list and use it for ongoing consultation as you begin to make decisions about how you might participate in public literacy.

Tracy and Pedro's list identified the following genres:

bumper stickers	grafitti
t-shirts	skywriting??
flyers	obituaries
memoranda	church marquee
sidewalk writing on campus	report
letter to the editor	license plates
headstones??	reward poster
sandwich board—"The End is Near"	buttons

In doing this exercise, Tracy discovered that many public literacy texts, particularly everyday public literacies, are so idiosyncratic that they defy genre classification. In her writer's notebook, Tracy recorded the example of a man driving around town with a house-shaped plywood sign in the back of his truck. In red, hand-painted letters, the man had written "Don't let this happen to you. I lost $10,000 because I bought my home from Heritage Homes. They ripped me off. They're cheaters." While certainly an example of public literacy—and arguably an issue in the public interest (consumer rights)—the text was probably one-of-a-kind.

Audience

In addition to *urgency*, rhetorical situations are composed of *audiences* and *constraints*, which we will discuss in this chapter. Considered together, these three components affect the choices you make regarding public literacy genres, public spheres, and the purposes of your writing.

An *audience* is a person or group of people to whom discourse is addressed. As with situations in general, not all audiences are rhetorical audiences.[1] In order to be "rhetorical," an audience must consist of people who are capable of two things: one, being influenced by the discourse directed toward them; and two, enacting proposed changes. In addition, audiences for public literacy must have access to the document you prepare (e.g., must be able to read the language in which it is written).

Unless it is composed of people who are utterly indifferent to the issue, have profound moral or ethical objections to the actions you propose, or are mentally disabled, an audience is generally receptive to suggestions for improving a situation. However, even those people who have been persuaded by your discourse might not be able—or willing—to take the actions you propose. For instance, criminals residing in federal penitentiaries might agree that one candidate would make the best president, but they are not allowed to vote. Other voters might agree that the candidate is the most qualified but be unconvinced that their vote will make any difference in the outcome of the election.

Clearly, audiences don't have to be convicted felons to be incapable of carrying out desired changes. Their capacity might also be affected by lack of transportation, limited financial resources, insufficient time, physical disability, moral or ethical objections, fear, apathy, age, different priorities, and a whole host of personal distractions. These factors need not disqualify audiences from hearing your message, but they might cause you to rethink your rhetorical goals.

The content and form of your writing are intimately influenced by who your audience is.[2] For example, if the goal of your writing were to encourage the President of the United States to allocate more money for student loans, you probably wouldn't put up flyers around campus (unless, of course, the President was visiting your campus). However, if your goal was to encourage *students* to put pressure on the President to do this, campus flyers might be an appropriate genre and public sphere. Since the purpose of public literacy is to set in motion actions in the public interest—or at least create in your audience a willingness to act at the appropriate time (e.g., vote in an election)—you need to be aware of what your audience regards as logical, true, fair, correct, and compelling.

But understanding your audience is often as challenging as it is necessary, for audiences, like rhetorical situations—and, indeed, like public spheres—are not fixed, stable entities. Even if it is friendly and familiar (perhaps made up of people like you), an audience is likely to be disorganized and multiform; thus it can't simply be "addressed" as if its members were sitting in a room together, politely waiting for you to tell them what to do (which hardly ever happens). Sometimes it is necessary to "invoke" an audience instead of addressing it—that is, create or summon the "ideal" audience.[3] As the Capitol Hill flyer in Chapter 2 illustrates, language can be a powerful means to do this: instead of saying "Attention, Police: Please Help Us!" (a strategy that had been ineffective), the flyer subtly *invokes* an audience of caring law enforcement officers who would assist the residents with their problem.

Constraints

Writers must also consider how their public literacy efforts might be undermined or *constrained*. *Constraints* describe any factors that complicate the writing of your document or an audience's reaction to it. They range from the very abstract (e.g., beliefs, values, motivations) to the very concrete (e.g., time, weather, money), from the minor (e.g., you don't have a magic marker) to the insurmountable (e.g., a tornado knocked the power out).

Although some mitigating circumstances can't be prevented, writers must try to anticipate as many constraints as possible so that they can revise their plans and goals accordingly. If you find yourself making excuses for why you can't engage in public literacy, the rhetorical situation you've identified probably isn't as urgent or as important to you as you originally thought.

Even circumstances that seem to lie outside the rhetorical situation can constrain public literacy efforts. Let's say, for example, that two days before student government elections, one candidate's staff posts flyers that feature a police mug shot of her opponent and the following message: "Is this the man you want handling your budget?" Maybe the accused candidate considers a response urgently important but has no money to create flyers or buy a radio spot. Or maybe he has three papers due that week, is sick, or thinks that his opponent's flyers won't really be that damaging. Thus external events and human judgments are introduced into the rhetorical situation, constraining possible responses.

Thinking Rhetorically

At this point, you have probably identified several urgent rhetorical situations that might be answered through public literacy. As you consider your options, generate a list of audiences that might find each rhetorical situation urgent (or that might be *persuaded* to find it urgent). Then for each audience, ask yourself the following questions:

1. Is the *audience* rhetorical?
    *   Are its members capable of being influenced by my writing?
    *   Are they capable of carrying out any actions I wish to propose?
    *   Can this audience be addressed or invoked through writing?

- Are its members likely to notice my document?
- Is my message likely to meet with their support?

If you answer "yes" to these questions, then make a list of public literacy genres that might be appropriate to your rhetorical situation (you should have a list in your writer's notebook). For each genre, ask yourself the following questions:

2. Is this *genre* suitable for this rhetorical situation?
   - Is it appropriate to my message?
   - Does my intended audience have access to it?
   - Is my audience likely to find it interesting and worthy of their attention?

If you also answer "yes" to these questions, then ask yourself:

3. Are there any *constraints* I can anticipate?
   - Do I have the time, commitment, and resources to create an appropriate public literacy document?
   - Do I have the skills necessary to create an appropriate document? If not, do I know anyone who has these skills, or can I obtain the skills in a timely fashion?
   - Do I have the knowledge and information about this *issue* to create an appropriate document? If not, am I willing and able to do the necessary research?
   - Do I have the knowledge and information about this *genre* to create an appropriate document? If not, am I willing and able to do the necessary research?
   - Do I have the knowledge and information about this *audience* to create an appropriate document? If not, am I willing and able to do the necessary research?
   - Am I willing to accept the risks and consequences of publishing my literacy document?

If the answers to all of these questions are "yes" or "maybe," then you have probably identified an audience and genre appropriate to your rhetorical situation, with few or minor constraints.

If the answer to any of these questions is "no," then you should work through the checklist again with different audiences, different genres, different goals—or different combinations of all of these. If you can't find a combination that seems to work, then you might want to reconsider whether to respond to this rhetorical situation, however urgent it might be. If the answer to any of these questions is "no" but you are committed to transforming the issue into a rhetorical situation that calls for public literacy, then you might need to rethink your goals or enlist a partner to assist you in your efforts.

Answering "no" to any of the items related to constraints does not necessarily mean that you should give up your plans to participate in public literacy. It simply means that you will face some challenges. If you are very interested in or committed to the issue, however, you can probably meet these challenges successfully. Carolyn McCarthy knew nothing about guns or politics until her husband was killed and her son seriously injured during a mass shooting on the Long Island Railroad in 1993. But she took the time and energy to find out, and now she's a member of the United States House of Representatives, using national public literacies to enact changes in laws regulating the ownership of assault weapons.

Exercise

In small groups, go back to the urgent rhetorical situation(s) you identified in Chapter 3. Then, work through the questions on the "Thinking Rhetorically" checklist above. By the end of this exercise, you should have at least one concrete plan for creating a public literacy document. Don't hesitate to think about rhetorical situations from multiple perspectives—to fit *your* motivations, commitments, skills, and beliefs. Remember, too, that plans are only "drafts," and can be revised as circumstances dictate.

Challenge yourself to identify several rhetorical situations every week. The more options you have, the more likely you are to find a situation that you want to respond to.

Let's return now to the rhetorical situation outlined by Pedro in Chapter 3. In response to a spate of nationally publicized school shootings, Pedro was concerned about school violence—more specifically, the need for parental involvement in students' lives, which Pedro believes could prevent such violence.

Pedro was initially skeptical about how writing might help to accomplish this ambitious goal, so in response to Tracy's advice, he set a more modest objective of teaching the parents of students in local schools how to be more involved in their children's lives. Pedro then made a list of local public spheres that dealt with parenting, schools, and violence; these included PTA and school board meetings, television news specials, talk radio, and school newsletters (some of which are written in several languages).

In response to the first two questions on the checklist, Pedro settled on the idea of publishing a regular column on effective parenting strategies in the school newsletters that were sent home with students every month. Upon further reflection, however, he recognized several constraints to his plan. Most seriously, he realized that although a parenting column might be a good idea and would likely reach his desired audience, he was neither qualified to write it nor able to become qualified in time to respond to this urgent rhetorical situation. This caused Pedro to reconsider his preliminary decisions regarding goals, audience, and genre. After working through the checklist a few more times, he eventually decided to write a letter to local school administrators, urging them to add a parenting column to their school newsletters.

At first glance, Pedro's plans may seem several steps removed from the problem of school violence—and indeed, Pedro himself might have envisioned a more "glamorous" response to the problem, such as spearheading a national movement for stricter gun control policies, or becoming a motivational speaker for high school students. But in reality, his goals are more likely to be effective because they are achievable, and when met, can encourage more ambitious efforts. It's worth remembering that public literacy doesn't have to garner a lot of attention or accolades to be successful. It only has to set realistic goals and reach the audience for whom it is intended.

Three Public Literacy Genres in Action

With so many possible combinations of urgency, audience, constraints, genres, and public spheres, it's not hard to understand why many writers abandon their public literacy goals in frustration. So let's look at an extended example of how the process of thinking rhetorically invites national, local, and everyday public literacies.

James Cooper and Chandler Snyder are avid bicyclists, but they were frustrated by the lack of safe bike lanes and convenient mass transit options in the city where they attend college, and also by the apparent lack of interest in a shuttle bus initiative designed to reduce the number of cars on campus. James and Chandler quickly concluded that these are indeed urgent rhetorical situations in the interest of their local public. They had a general sense of their goals—to improve alternative transportation options in the city and on campus—and brainstormed several more specific solutions before deciding to proceed:

participate in Critical Mass rides

ask City Council (Department of Transportation?) to build bike lanes

start a Yellow Bike program

see if there are any tax breaks for cities that invest in alternative transportation infrastructure

write letters to editors of school and local paper encouraging them to use the shuttle

distribute maps of existing bike routes in city (also shuttle schedules?)

public service announcements—raise awareness about biking or campus shuttle?

work for candidates who support the building of bike lanes

e-mail campaign?

James and Chandler realized that several of their ideas represented *physical* rather than *rhetorical* actions. In particular, they were concerned that Critical Mass rides (where large groups of bicyclists clog streets during rush hours to protest dependency on cars) might be construed as annoying expressions of self-interest rather than persuasive calls for action. They thought they might be able to promote such actions through writing, but agreed that these solutions were less likely to influence non-cyclists.

After working through the "Thinking Rhetorically" checklists, James and Chandler decided that they wanted to start a Yellow Bike program—where bikes are painted yellow and left around a city or campus, unlocked, for common use. They anticipated several constraints, including lack of money and bikes, but mapped out a four-step process that they hoped would allow them to establish the program gradually: first, collect as many donated bikes as possible; second, obtain funding to refurbish and paint the bikes and promote the program; third, organize a group of people to maintain the bikes and monitor the success of the program; and finally, obtain funding to expand the program to the local community.

1. Everyday Public Literacies

In order to solicit donations for the Yellow Bike program and encourage others to join their efforts, Chandler and James, with the help of supportive friends, created and posted flyers at local bike stores and second-hand stores and on community bulletin boards; using a campus-wide e-mail distribution list, they sent messages to all faculty and staff; on weekends, they combed rummage sales and salvage yards. Their efforts yielded them 38 donated bikes—some nearly new, others in various states of disrepair.

Chandler, James, and their friends represent an informal network of people engaged in purposeful public literacy work (as well as physical effort). Although their goals are designed to serve a broader public interest—that is, to benefit people other than themselves, including people they don't know—no one is monitoring or controlling their efforts. Significantly, the public spheres where they chose to publicize their project required little or no financial investment on their part.

2. Local Public Literacies

Because they believed their project would improve the lives of the entire campus community, Chandler and James decided to ask their Student Government Association for money to paint and refurbish the bikes they had collected. They picked up a copy of the SGA "Special Activity Fund Request Form and Guidelines" (see Chapter 10), at which point they encountered their first major obstacle: the application required

Chandler and James to list the name of their campus organization and the number of members, but they hadn't yet formed an organization.

So Chandler and James revised their original plan, arranging a meeting for everyone who had donated bikes or expressed interest in their project. At this meeting, the group decided to call themselves SCAT—"Students and Community for Alternative Transportation"—and drafted a mission statement that articulated its goals and ideals. Chandler and James then filled out the Special Activity Fund application on behalf of SCAT, submitted the necessary copies, and presented their proposal to the SGA Appropriations Committee, who awarded the group $500.

Just because Chandler and James established a formal organization doesn't mean that SCAT can no longer participate in everyday public literacies. Indeed, grassroots organizing and everyday literacies might be the most effective means to accomplish their goals. However, most everyday publics exist within local contexts—institutions, traditions, even prejudices specific to a geographical place—that both enable and constrain public literacy efforts. Engaging in local public literacies often obligates writers to accept institutional procedures and writing conventions.

3. National Public Literacies

James and Chandler were satisfied with obtaining some funding to launch the Yellow Bike program and SCAT on campus. With an eye toward expanding the program, they applied for nonprofit or "501(c)(3)" status, which, among other things, exempted SCAT's tiny budget from federal taxation and entitled the group to reduced postal rates. The incorporation process was long and confusing, and involved filling out several federal forms, revising SCAT's mission statement, and establishing bylaws and a board of directors.

National public literacies make it legal for James and Chandler to undertake every idea on their original list, if they so choose. The First Amendment, for example, guarantees their right to participate in peaceful Critical Mass rides, or distribute documents promoting their ideas.

But some national documents, such as those James filled out to establish SCAT as a nonprofit corporation, do more than make public literacy possible: they actually encourage it by providing a national public sphere, or by offering resources, support, and legal protection to members of a national public. Some of these literacies—such as the IRS publication "Application for Recognition of Exemption," which details eligibility requirements and procedures for applying for federal tax exempt status—are sponsored by the federal government, but many are made available by groups or organizations working in the national public interest.

Establishing the Yellow Bike program on campus was not as easy as it might sound here; it took several months, and Chandler and James encountered many obstacles along the way. Their efforts were further constrained by the fact that they are both serious students with a variety of other interests and commitments. At the same time, their actions provide a good example of how public literacy can intervene in a specific problem on many levels.

Notes

1. The sections on audience and constraints are influenced by Lloyd F. Bitzer's article, "The Rhetorical Situation" (*Philosophy and Rhetoric* 1 [1968]: 1–14).

2. The ideas in this paragraph come from Walter R. Fisher's book, *Human Communication as Narration* (Columbia: U of South Carolina P, 1987), and Chaim Perelman and L. Olbrechts-Tyteca's book, *The New Rhetoric: A Treatise on Argumentation* (Notre Dame, IN: U of Notre Dame P, 1969).

3. Ede, Lisa, and Andrea Lunsford. "Audience Addressed/Audience Invoked: The Role of Audience in Composition Theory and Pedagogy." *College Composition and Communication* 35 (1984): 155–71.

CHAPTER 5

Research in the Public Interest

There may be times when you have to do additional research in order to respond to a rhetorical situation effectively. The nature of that research will depend upon the rhetorical situation. For example, if an urgent rhetorical situation requires an immediate response, you may not have time to pore over archival documents or interview several people; this may in turn constrain your choice of audience and genre. In other situations, though, lack of knowledge or information can actually inspire your participation in public literacy.

National public literacy documents apply equally to all members of that public, and are generally accessible to all *readers*; however, they are usually *written* by a small minority of people within that diverse public sphere. Conversely, everyday public literacy documents are accessible to all readers and writers within a social or political network but circulate with little oversight and so have few hard-and-fast "rules." For these reasons, this chapter will focus on research in the local public sphere, including how to use local sources, how to gain "insider knowledge" about a community, and how to translate academic knowledge into local contexts.

Local Knowledge

Sometimes the concept of a public sphere can seem so abstract and complex as to be incomprehensible—and hence inaccessible. In such circumstances, it can be useful to turn our attention to *local knowledge*: what "everybody knows" about a community, like what the "good schools" and "bad neighborhoods" are, or where to get the freshest produce. Like everyday public literacies, local knowledge is informal and largely uncontrolled by official institutions. It describes what is recognized as true, correct, and worthwhile by a community, and the ways in which those beliefs are influenced by histories, memories, traditions, and language within a specific geographical setting.[1] Paying attention to local knowledge can enrich our understanding of cultural practices such as public literacy and increase our opportunities to participate in them effectively.

Even in the smallest, most apparently homogeneous communities, local knowledges are negotiated by various public and private actions, special interest groups, and texts. The more diverse a community, the more likely that its history, values, and beliefs will be contested. Many residents might agree on the "bad neighborhoods," for example, but have very different perspectives on *why* a neighborhood is considered "bad," how it came to be "bad" in the first place, and who's responsible for improving it. These perspectives are not always debated openly or amicably; some interests may be represented more conspicuously or more favorably in public discourse, and others may not be represented at all. In fact, local knowledge is often unspoken—something people "just know," but don't talk about or write down.

At the same time, much local knowledge is mediated by written language, whether through national or local literacies (e.g., laws), everyday literacies, or professional literacies like advertising and journalism. Members of a local public who can read and write regularly use language to engage with and make sense of the world—often so unconsciously that we take it for granted. We read newspapers and write letters to editors, we file insurance claims and appeal hospital charges, we vote and work to elect candidates whose platforms we support. Such actions allow us not just to acquire local knowledge, but to actively create it. In doing so we become shareholders in local knowledge, using literacy to empower ourselves and others.

Local knowledge does have its limitations. Because it is situated in a specific time and place, it may offer few insights into the culture practices of other communities, even those that appear to be similar. Moreover, because it evolves over time, it's virtually impossible to grasp local knowledge fully, especially if you're a new resident. And yet, local knowledge is part of the full matrix of intellectual life within a community, and its significance can't be disregarded.

Of course, there's no "Book of Local Knowledge" to demystify all this. But research can offer insight into local knowledge as well as mobilize it in the public interest.

Three Approaches to Local Research

I. Consulting Local Sources

Every day we encounter texts, sites, services, and artifacts that are so ordinary and familiar that we might underestimate them as sources of information. These local sources include:

Local newspapers	Newscasts	Radio broadcasts
Telephone books and directories	Library collections	Agency brochures
Festivals and other events	Laws and ordinances	Landmarks
Maps and guidebooks	Local museum exhibits	Local fact books

While almost all communities make some of these sources available to the local public—often at no cost—the information contained within them is specific to each setting and contributes to a body of local knowledge that is virtually unique.

Local sources can reveal much about the character of a place, in ways that range from the whimsical to the weighty. For example, signs at the outskirts of Central City, Nebraska, promote that city as "Pump Irrigation Center of the World," while signs at the outskirts of Wilmington proclaim "Incorporated 1739" and "Home of the North Carolina Azalea Festival." Such information is more than merely interesting: it also offers insight into what these communities value, how they define themselves, and what they consider to be in the public interest.

The depth, timeliness, and accuracy of local source materials varies widely. Some, like daily newspapers, are able to provide up-to-date and detailed analysis of current events, while others, such as maps, generally offer little or no interpretation and may become outdated within months.

Even relatively superficial sources can be rich sources of local information. Consider telephone books: simply looking through the government "blue pages" can not only expand your understanding of government duties, but also introduce you to bureaucratic structures. Phone books can guide you to government offices and nonprofit or philanthropic organizations, many of which provide literature to community residents at no charge. This information can, in turn, assist you in researching issues in the public interest and making informed choices about how to participate in public literacy.

Many local sources represent official perspectives designed to provide members of a local public (including tourists or other non-residents) with information and give them a sense of shared identity. This is not to say, however, that local sources offer a single version of local knowledge that everyone accepts as true. In fact, they may tell conflicting stories, thus revealing tensions in local knowledge and leaving you with more questions than answers about a community. Local knowledge is defined as much by what local sources exclude as by what they include, which is why it's important to read them critically.

Sometimes local knowledge can be found in national sources. If you want to find demographic information about a community (e.g., statistics related to race, age, income, education, pet ownership, housing costs, bankruptcies filed), the following sources—all published annually—are good places to start[2]:

Print Sources:

Statistical Abstract of the United States. U. S. Bureau of the Census. Washington, DC: GPO. A wide range of economic, social, and political statistics, gleaned mostly from government sources.

World Almanac and Book of Facts. Mahwah, NJ: Funk & Wagnalls. Published since 1868; a good source for current and historical information.

Information Please, Almanac, Atlas and Yearbook. Boston: Houghton Mifflin. Contains information on popular culture in addition to statistics.

Facts on File: A Weekly World News Digest. New York: Facts on File. Published twice monthly; timely source for current events.

On-line Sources:

Statistical Abstract:
    http://www.census.gov/stat_abstract/
    Not as extensive as the print version.

Census Bureau:
    http://www.census.gov/main/www/subjects.html
    Statistical information organized by subject.

Almanac of American Politics:
    http://politicsusa.com/PoliticsUSA/resources/almanac/
    Information about contemporary federal and state politics and politicians.

Exercise

Do a *content analysis* of a local newspaper: a detailed list of topics, issues, themes, and perspectives represented within it. To do this, skim every issue for at least a month, focusing on front page headlines; any section whose focus is local, regional, or "neighborhood" news; and the opinion pages, including letters to the editor. In your writer's notebook, make a list of recurring themes, names of people who are mentioned repeatedly, ongoing local debates, and so on, recording the number of references. As you do your content analysis, take note of other newspaper features that might reflect local values—for example, special interest pages or columns, comic strips, and the proportion of locally-written versus syndicated material.

Now do a content analysis of at least one other kind of local source—the phone book, for example, or a visitors' guide. If your community publishes more than one newspaper—an "alternative" weekly, for example—you may also choose to analyze this source, comparing and contrasting it to a more "mainstream" newspaper.

Then, in small groups, consolidate your content analyses, and see if you can come up with a composite description of your local community. In general, what are the people like? What do they seem to care about, value, enjoy?

What bothers them? What unites and divides them? How do they character-ize themselves? What groups are strongly represented in local public dis-course? What groups are underrepresented or invisible? What issues or per-spectives get talked about a lot, not much, or not at all? What tensions in local knowledge can you observe? What questions emerge from these ten-sions or contradictions?

Pedro initially found this exercise difficult because he lives in the Washing-ton, D.C., area, where the local culture is often indistinguishable from the national culture of government, the museums of the Smithsonian Institu-tion, and a host of national landmarks. Even the "local newspaper"–the *Washington Post*–enjoys a national circulation. Tracy suggested that Pedro search for less prominent local sources, such as suburban newspapers and phone books, that serve more distinct local publics.

If you live in a very large, cosmopolitan, or nationally prominent city like Pe-dro, it may be more fruitful for you to think of it as composed of many local publics. If this proves too difficult, you might want to use local sources to try to define a national public: by reading locally published newspapers with na-tional circulations, visiting local museums of national culture, and so on, what conclusions can you draw about what this country values? What stories does our country like to tell about itself? What issues and perspectives does it consider important or marginal? What gaps, tensions, or conflicts do na-tional sources reveal?

Tracy's response to the exercises appear later in this chapter.

2. Gaining "Insider Knowledge"

In the book *Midnight in the Garden of Good and Evil*, writer John Berendt runs across a reference to "Sadie Jefferson" in a 1914 Savannah newspaper and later looks in the city directory to find out who this woman was. When he finds no record of her, a librarian takes one look at his newspaper clipping and immediately informs him that he has consulted the wrong part of the directory. Noting that the courtesy title "Miss" or "Mrs." had been omitted from the reference, the librarian concluded that Sadie Jeffer-son was African American, and thus would be listed in the "Colored" section of the city directory.[3]

Berendt wasn't even aware that there *was* a "Colored" section of the directory. But the bigger lesson to be learned from this experience is that local knowledge is more than the sum of its parts–more, in other words, than a list of phone numbers, names, dates, and historical sites. Making sense of these bits and pieces of information often requires more than the official interpretations provided by local public literacy sources. It can require the "insider knowledge" of people who have lived in a community for a long time—a deeply contextualized understanding of what characterizes it as a place. Usually we develop this kind of knowledge over time, as we live in a community and learn its conventions and idiosyncracies. There are ways to expedite this process, however, and one of these is to interview longtime residents.[4]

Choosing an Informant

The purpose of this type interview is to gain insights that aren't available elsewhere, particularly those that community "outsiders" do not yet have the resources to understand. Longtime residents of a community make ideal informants, particularly if they can offer perspectives that are not well represented in local public documents. You may already know some people who would be good sources of insider knowledge. If you don't, neighbors, friends, professors, and family members may be able to suggest good informants, as can the Advancement Office or Alumni Association at your college.

Even if you already possess an insider's understanding of your community's local knowledge, you can still learn from an interview. Talking to a longtime resident who has experienced the community differently than you have—because of differences in physical ability or socioeconomic status, for example—will surely yield fresh insights into local knowledge.

The most important criteria when choosing informants is that they have an interest in your subject and a willingness to talk to you. Another important consideration, however, is maturity. A teenager who has lived in the same community his whole life will certainly possess significant insider knowledge. An older person, however, might be more experienced at reflecting on his knowledge and connecting it to larger networks of information and experience. (This varies from informant to informant, of course.)

Asking Good Questions

It's vital that you prepare your questions and review them carefully in advance so that you can devote your full attention to your informant during the interview. Crafting good questions can be difficult, but a good way to get started is to make a list of reasons why you are interested in talking to your informant, and then use this list to develop your initial questions. For example, if you chose your informant because she was active in local government for many years, you might ask her how she became involved in politics. These kinds of questions can introduce you to interesting personal and local histories as well as set the tone of your interview. They can also steer your informant away from answers that are superficial or uncritical, or that simply parrot the Chamber of Commerce version of local knowledge.

Since the goal of your interview is to gain insider knowledge, you should ask questions that invite your informant to reflect on and interpret information. Questions that begin with "Why" or "How" can facilitate this process, while questions that elicit simple "yes" or "no" answers do not. If you don't understand an answer or want to know more, ask follow-up questions: "Why is that?" "Can you explain what you mean?" "I'd like to go back to something you said earlier. . . ." Needless to say, you should never interrupt or argue with an informant; wait for an appropriate time to ask follow-up questions, and offer your own opinions only when your informant solicits them.

During the interview, your most important role is to listen carefully to what your informant is saying. Simply put: your informant should be doing most of the talking. Don't worry if they don't respond right away. If you ask good questions, they might need some time to think about their answers.

Interview Etiquette
Not all interviews will go smoothly: some informants may be shy, reserved, or self-conscious; you might even be nervous yourself. Still, you can make the most of an interview by coming prepared, listening attentively, and being flexible if the interview takes an unexpected turn. If possible, ask a partner to review your questions and practice the interview with you ahead of time so that you are comfortable listening and taking notes at the same time. It can also be helpful to give your informant a copy of the questions before the interview so that they will have time to think through their answers; this can help you avoid uncomfortable silences or unfocused answers during the interview.

Although people who grant you interviews are important local sources, you can't treat them as you might the local library or history museum. In other words, you can't simply show up at their door, ask them some questions off the top of your head, and leave. Always schedule the interview as far in advance as possible and confirm your appointment. Be sure to arrive on time and dress conservatively; come prepared with a list of questions, your writer's notebook, writing utensils, and, if possible, a tape recorder. After the interview, write or call your informant to thank them for sharing their time and knowledge with you, and offer to give them a copy of any writing that makes use of their contribution.

Exercise

Go back to the content analyses of local sources that you recorded in your writer's notebook, and identify information that you found confusing or contradictory. Then ask around for names of community insiders who could help you to interpret this information; record these names in your writer's notebook. Arrange to interview at least one of these people with the purpose of enhancing your own local knowledge. You may wish to focus your interview on collecting stories about what your community used to be like or how it has changed over the years. Or you may wish to take advantage of this opportunity to gain insights into the questions you raised in your content analyses.

Prepare a draft of your interview questions in advance, and ask a partner to read them with an eye toward revision.

3. Translating Academic Research

Local knowledge can be more meaningful within the context of the larger world of people, events, and ideas that you are learning about in school—and vice versa. There will probably be many instances where you feel that a local public would benefit from academic knowledge, perhaps because it can shed light on or even provide solutions to local problems in the public interest. Sharing academic research can be a responsible way to contribute to local knowledge, but it can also be a bit tricky.

Whenever you use research to enhance the persuasiveness of your writing, it is absolutely vital that you consult the kinds of sources that will be valued by your audience, and use these sources according to conventions your audience expects and understands. In an academic setting, your audience will primarily consist of college professors, most of whom value some form of academic research—that is, the kind found in professional books and journals and which includes theoretical discussions, experimental data, and interpretations offered by other experts with academic credentials. Academic research writing conventions vary from discipline to discipline. However, much of the writing and research you will be asked to do in college is designed to introduce you to these conventions so that you will be able to use them skillfully in college and your career.

When writing public literacy documents, however, you almost never rely on the disciplinary jargon and documentation conventions you practice in college. These features of academic writing represent a kind of shorthand: not only do people who write in academic settings understand what these features signify, but they recognize their users as academic insiders—people who have subject matter knowledge and have been socialized into the conventions of their discipline. People who read and write outside of an academic context may find such conventions confusing, unnecessary, or even pretentious.

Likewise, a local public audience may prefer some sources or genres over others—for example, local histories written by amateur historians rather than those written by professors using obscure theories and documents, or informational brochures rather than academic articles. The problem is not simply that a public audience might find these sources difficult to understand; it's that they might feel that academic knowledge obscures rather than illuminates local issues. It is the responsibility of the writer to anticipate these possible constraints before creating a public document.

It's vital that you regard "translating" research for local audiences as a process of making knowledge more accessible, not "dummying it down." Many important public discussions have been derailed because local audiences perceive academic experts as arrogant and remote, a perception that understandably causes resentment and does little to promote cooperation in the public interest. Making specialized knowledge accessible to a non-specialist audience is a sign of courtesy as well as authority. When translating research, try to keep in mind situations in which someone has had to explain unfamiliar information to you—cooking, for example, or the stock market. What strategies did they use to make that information comprehensible and relevant?

While universities contribute to both academic knowledge and local knowledge, they are also geographically specific communities themselves, and thus have their own bodies of local knowledge: who the hardest professors are, when the cafeteria is least crowded, and so on. Researching the local knowledge of your university can reveal urgent rhetorical situations as well as novel opportunities for intervening in them. While campus directories, catalogs, and newspapers are excellent sources for such knowledge, less prominent university publications (e.g., budgets) and local, state, and national records (e.g., tax returns) can reveal such information as your university's investment portfolio, faculty salaries and research contracts, and any lawsuits filed against your school.

Most of this information is fairly easy to find at a public university, and indeed, the Freedom of Information Act (FOIA) and other laws guarantee you access to it. If information is seen as politically sensitive, however, you may have difficulty obtaining it. Texts such as *Raising Hell: A Citizen's Guide to the Fine Art of Investigation*, can help you to navigate this process successfully.[5]

Local Research in Action

For her local research, Tracy did content analyses of two local newspapers during approximately the same period: the *Wilmington Morning Star*, which is published daily, and the *Wilmington Journal*, a weekly publication with a primarily African American readership. She wrote down every topic that appeared at least three times during a month, with additional marks for additional mentions. Her lists appear below:

Wilmington Morning Star (April 15–May 15, 1999)

war in Yugoslavia (12)

beach replenishment (9); Shell Island (8)

school safety post-Columbine (9); gun control (8)

taxes (8)

city-county consolidation (7)

community college issues—growing enrollment, expansion, proposal to make main street pedestrian only (6)

hog farms, pollution control (6)

middle school trip to Disney World—educational value (5)

budget crisis at Hospice (5)

School Board debate on school uniforms (5)

city storm water drainage—fees, flooding issues (5)

the removal of B.C. from the comics section (5)

crime rate in Brunswick County—robberies up (4)

protection of wetlands (4)

parking issues and traffic at beach (4)

racist remark by university trustee (3)

zoning issues (3)

neglect of drama room at high school (3)

NC strawberries—in season; some infected with anthracnose which rots them (3)

lack of support for teaching Spanish in county schools (3)

sex offender registration (3)

Wilmington Journal (April–May, 1999)

racial distribution of county teachers (9)

school violence/safety (7)

Jesse Jackson—rescue of POWs, debate with Jesse Helms (6)

"driving-while-black" (5)

school uniforms (3)

NAACP increases membership fees (3)

NATO/war issues (3)

lack of major accomplishments by NC Black Caucus (3)

fair housing issues (3)

racist remark by university trustee—students want apology (3)

[African American] high school student Anthony Kelly arrested for making bomb threats on Internet (3)

support for [African American sheriff] Joe McQueen (3)

black farmers—additional support money needed (3)

black media needs support (3)

Azalea Festival boycott (3)

After doing this exercise, Tracy was struck by the fact that the *Journal* and the *Morning Star* published very little of the same news, and when they did, they usually brought radically different perspectives to their articles and editorials. She was particularly disturbed to find that the issue that received the most attention in the *Journal* during the period of her analysis—racial distribution of teachers in county schools—received absolutely no coverage in the *Morning Star*, and that the issues discussed most frequently in the *Morning Star*—war, school safety, and various local government issues—received little or no coverage in the *Journal*. Tracy also noted that the proposed Azalea Festival boycott somewhat undermined the cheerful "Home of the North Carolina Azalea Festival" message that welcomed visitors to the city.

These observations led Tracy to conclude that the African American and white populations of Wilmington were sharply divided in terms of what they thought was important and newsworthy. She wondered whether African American residents feel like they have a stake in local government, and whether white residents feel concerned about issues primarily affecting their black neighbors. Tracy then consulted the original list of interests and concerns that she compiled in her writer's notebook (Chapter 1), and realized that with the exception of several articles related to the environmental impact of urban development, none of the issues on this list were represented in either publication.

Tracy also noticed that the *Wilmington Journal* proclaims on its editorial masthead that it is "Founded on the Principles of the Black Press Creed," which holds that "America can best lead the world away from racial and national antagonisms when it accords to every person, regardless of race, color, or creed, full human and legal rights[, h]ating no person in the firm belief that all are hurt as long as anyone is held back." Since the *Morning Star* avows no such policy, Tracy speculated that the *Journal* might function at least in part as an advocacy publication for the local African American population.

Taking her cue from the *Journal* article about the NAACP, Tracy decided to set up an interview with an officer in the local chapter, whom she located by visiting the African American Cultural Center on her campus and consulting the local telephone book. Among other things, Tracy learned from her interview that many African American residents of Wilmington subscribe to both the *Morning Star* and the *Journal* because they see both perspectives as important, but that since the *Journal* operates on a limited budget it can't afford a "newspapers in education" program that places it in the public schools. (It is available locally in all municipal and academic libraries.)

Reflecting on this information, Tracy recalled a paper she had written for a "Politics of Literacy" class, drawing upon the theories of Brazilian educator Paulo Freire. Freire believed that people become not just literate but also politically conscious through the use of language and concepts that matter in their everyday lives. Tracy wondered whether African American students had adequate opportunities to develop as vital, literate citizens if the newspaper that best represented their interests was not available in the schools.

Tracy was convinced that the discrepancies between local "mainstream" and "black" news suggested several urgent rhetorical situations, including a possible shortage of relevant information and literacy development opportunities for many local residents. She knew, however, that it would be inappropriate to send a copy of the paper she wrote for her theory class to the *Morning Star*. Instead, Tracy listed several other possible actions she might take in order to call attention to the situation:

organize a public roundtable discussion of race and the media

write a letter to the editor of the *Morning Star* requesting more news coverage relevant to African Americans

picket the newspaper offices

raise money to purchase *Journal* subscriptions for local schools

After working through the "Thinking Rhetorically" checklists in Chapters 3 and 4, Tracy decided to pursue the last idea on her list. We'll revisit her efforts in Chapter 8.

Notes

1. This section is influenced by David Barton and Mary Hamilton's *Local Literacies: Reading and Writing in One Community* (London: Routledge, 1998) and Clifford Geertz's *Local Knowledge: Further Essays in Interpretive Anthropology* (New York: Basic, 1983).

2. This annotated list comes from Bruce Ballenger's book *The Curious Researcher: A Guide to Writing Research Papers* (2nd. ed. Boston: Allyn & Bacon, 1998. 204–7).

3. Berendt, John. *Midnight in the Garden of Good and Evil: A Savannah Story*. New York: Random House, 1994. 26, 42.

4. Readers seeking more detailed information on conducting interviews should consult Cynthia Stokes Brown's book *Like It Was: A Complete Guide to Writing Oral History* (New York: Teachers & Writers Collaborative, 1988), which informs much of this section.

5. Noyes, Dan. *Raising Hell: A Citizen's Guide to the Fine Art of Investigation*. San Francisco: Center for Investigative Reporting, 1983.

CHAPTER 6

Focus on Letters

Letters represent one of the most common public literacy genres—and one of the most versatile. Among other things, letters can express opinions, rally support for an idea, offer praise or censure, ask for money, and request information. Of course, letters serve many other purposes besides public ones (e.g., personal correspondence), and those that appear in the public sphere are not necessarily in the public interest. But their ability to reach a broad audience while still sounding personal makes them an ideal genre choice for a variety of rhetorical situations.

Ironically, it's because letters are such a familiar genre that some writers have a hard time thinking of them as public literacy texts. While most letters share some basic conventions—a greeting and closing, a signature—the specific content, form, and tone of a letter are determined by its purpose. Although this chapter is not a "how-to" guide, it will sketch the rhetorical contours of four types of letters commonly used for public purposes: letters to editors of publications, letters of concern, appeal letters, and open letters.

Letters to the Editor

Letters to the editor of a publication generally comment on material that appears in that publication. Sometimes these letters add or clarify information, or offer a different perspective; in such cases, an urgent rhetorical situation is occasioned by incorrect, biased, or incomplete information. Often, writers use letters to question editorial decisions—some major, some relatively minor. For example, when one local newspaper stopped running the comic strip *Shoe*, many readers protested in the form of letters to the editor, and the strip was reinstated. In these cases, the rhetorical situation is considered urgent because of a perceived lapse in editorial judgment that writers regard as correctable through discourse.

Some letters to the editor might be more accurately described as letters to *readers* of a publication. For example, in some local newspapers it's not unusual to read a letter like this one: "The John Smith who was arrested for drunk driving on March 1 was not the John Smith that lives at 503 East 18th Street." In this case, it was readers of the newspaper, not editors, who composed the rhetorical audience—that is, the audience capable of acting on the information in the letter (e.g., by continuing to patronize Mr. Smith's business). The editors are also a rhetorical audience in this situation, however: as the *gatekeepers* of the public interest, it was they who decided to publish the letter.

It can be useful when writing a letter to the editor to mention any special experience or credentials that make you an expert on the issue you are addressing. Sometimes, though, this information reveals possible conflicts of interest. For example, a self-identified physician wrote a letter to the editor of a magazine in response to an article on the popularity of alternative healing methods such as acupuncture. She compared practitioners of these methods to snake-oil salesmen and urged readers to consult medical doctors for serious health problems. Certainly, this doctor's education and professional experience give her some amount of authority on this subject, and indeed, she might have felt ethically obligated to express her professional opinion in this situation. But she might also have a financial stake in steering readers away from alternative healers, a possibility which somewhat undermines her message.

Most letters columns feature submission guidelines, including recommended length, postal and e-mail addresses for submitting letters, and so on. These guidelines may constrain your writing to some extent, but it is wise to follow them carefully, for letters that don't meet the guidelines might be summarily rejected, regardless of the content. If a letter is too long to publish, the editors might revise it themselves, in which case you run the risk of having your ideas distorted or important information deleted.

When you submit a letter to the editor, you are usually required not only to sign your name but also to include your address and phone number so that the editorial staff can verify that you wrote the letter before they publish it. This practice exists primarily to hold writers accountable for the opinions they express publicly. If people were not required to sign their names, they would be free to make outrageous or inaccurate claims—anonymously or in someone else's name.

The features of a good letter to the editor vary widely, which is why you should always look at letters columns in target publications for models. In general, though, letters should address a matter in the public interest, have a clear point, be accurate, and convey a calm, sensible tone. They should demonstrate understanding and respect for the cultural and educational sensibilities of readers and avoid insulting or inflammatory language, name-calling, and intentional deception. Finally, they should be conscientiously revised and edited. Your letter might still be published even if it doesn't meet these criteria, but it has a better chance of influencing both editors and readers if it does.

Exercise

Find letters columns in several of the following kinds of publications: student newspaper, local daily or weekly newspaper, national newspaper (e.g., *USA Today*), weekly or monthly general interest magazine (e.g., *TIME, Smithsonian*), popular culture magazine (e.g., *People*), special interest magazine or newspaper (e.g., *Outside, Baseball Weekly*), academic journal, and on-line magazine (e.g., *Slate*).

Then, in small groups, compare and contrast the submission guidelines for each publication and the characteristics of the letters they publish. What accounts for these similarities and differences? Are there some letters that seem "better" than others? If so, why?

Newspapers and magazines suggest innumerable rhetorical situations. Some may inspire you to write letters to the editor, but others may inform you of urgent situations that you could respond to through other public literacy genres or actions. Challenge yourself to read a local or national newspaper several times a week, recording potential rhetorical situations in your writer's notebook.

Letters of Concern

Letters of concern are generally directed toward individuals for the purpose of seeking assistance, improving a situation, or solving a problem. What distinguishes them from letters of *complaint* is that they try to propose actions or solutions rather than simply identify problems. Of course, sometimes we experience urgent problems that we don't know how to solve. Often, though, we know how our situations could be improved, but just need to forward our ideas to a rhetorical audience—that is, a person or persons capable of carrying them out.

Because letters of concern are generally sent to individuals, they aren't "public" in the sense that all members of a national, local, or everyday public have access to them as *readers*. However, such letters often address issues in the public interest, and the genre is available to all members of a public as *writers*. Public officials often make good rhetorical audiences; their postal and e-mail addresses and phone and fax numbers are readily available on-line, at libraries, and at many government offices.

Like letters to the editor, letters of concern are more likely to reach their intended audience if they conform to certain basic conventions. Since traditional business letters are among the most formal of letter genres, they cannot convey the seriousness of your concern as well as invoke an audience who takes your ideas seriously.

Although there are many different kinds of business letters, they are generally brief (ideally, no more than one page) and get to the point quickly; they specify problems and solutions directly, and establish the writer's relationship to the recipient (including the recipient's obligations, if any, to the writer) at the outset. The tone of a letter of concern should be polite but earnest. As with letters to the editor, the writer should make every effort to provide accurate, relevant information, and be mindful of the interests of their audience.

Business letter format varies widely as well, but the most formal are written in "block style" (left margins flush, no indentations) and include these features:

Date: month (spelled out), day, year

Address: the same address that appears on the envelope, including recipient's name and appropriate title of office (e.g., Dr. Gail Womble, Principal)

Greeting: "Dear —" (title and last name) followed by a colon; letters of complaint should ideally be directed toward a specific person, but if this is not possible, use a generic description such as "Dear Principal"

Body: short paragraphs, with two spaces between each paragraph

> *first paragraph* (1–2 sentences): establishes relationship to recipient and purpose for writing

> *middle paragraphs*: elaborate on request (e.g., by providing evidence of problem, and describing prior efforts to seek assistance and possible benefits of proposed actions)

> *final paragraph* (1–2 sentences): reiterates the urgency of the situation and asks recipient to take specific action

Closing: "Yours truly" or some similar phrase, followed by a comma

Signature: your name, signed in ink; leave three lines between closing and your typewritten name

Enclosures: "encl."; an optional feature which indicates that additional materials (e.g., receipts) are included with your letter

Copies: "cc" followed by a colon and names of any other recipients, listed in alphabetical order; optional

These conventions can be adapted to meet the needs of less formal rhetorical situations—for example, by indenting paragraphs and moving the date and closing to the right (see "Appeal Letters" below).

Exercise

Look through the problems and concerns you have listed in your writer's notebook and select one or two that seem particularly important to you. Then, brainstorm several possible solutions or improvements, and several rhetorical audiences to whom you might address letters of concern. If the rhetorical situation is urgent and a letter of concern seems like an appropriate genre with which to respond to it, write your letter, ask a partner to read it with an eye toward possible revisions, and send it.

On the next page, you will see the letter that Pedro drafted to send to the principal of his brother's school, expressing his concerns about school violence and proposing an action that could improve the safety of students and staff. Consult the criteria for effective letters of concern and the peer review questions listed at the end of this chapter, then read the letter carefully. What suggestions would you offer Pedro as he undertakes his revisions?

June 30, 1999

Dr. Gail Womble, Principal
Rachel Carson Middle School
13618 McLearen Rd.
Herndon, VA 20170

Dear Dr. Womble:

As a recent graduate of Fairfax County Public Schools, and the brother of a student currently attending Rachel Carson Middle School, I am concerned about school safety.

In the wake of the recent school shootings in Littleton, Colorado, and elsewhere, many important issues regarding the causes of school violence have risen to the public's conscience. Numerous people have blamed the shooters' parents for their actions, and while the validity of this point may be in dispute, the fact remains that there are many adults who do not know how to communicate effectively with their children or recognize the warning signs that their children are troubled. If parents had accessible means of receiving parenting advice, perhaps tragedies like the one in Littleton could be avoided.

Since not all parents can afford to subscribe to parenting magazines or consult counselors, I believe that schools should take a more active role in promoting good parenting skills. Perhaps the most efficient way of accomplishing this would be to add a parenting column to the monthly newsletter that the school already sends to all parents.

It would not take much effort or money to publish such a column. In fact, some counselor or psychologist might be willing to do it for free, and if you started planning right away, you could have the column in place by the time school starts in the fall. But regardless of the cost or effort, the benefits of a parenting column could be incalculable. Imagine, schools could be safer and child-parent relationships could be better, too.

I hope that you will consider this suggestion with the utmost of urgency so that we can prevent such terrible episodes of school violence from ever reaching Rachel Carson Middle School.

Respectfully yours,

Pedro Marques

cc: Fairfax County Board of Education

Appeal Letters

Appeal letters are sent to mass audiences on behalf of individuals or organizations. Because their purpose is usually to raise money or increase membership, they are often used by political candidates or parties and nonprofit groups like the Nature Conservancy or the March of Dimes. Appeal letters should be distinguished from *solicitation* letters, such as credit card or magazine subscription offers, whose purpose is primarily to make money rather than promote some public interest.

Appeal letters usually arrive in the mail and may include a postage-paid return envelope. But there are other ways of sending appeal letters, too. For example, groups like the Surfrider Foundation, which is devoted to beach conservation and water quality monitoring, rely on e-mail distribution lists to send appeal letters at no cost. While this strategy saves money and paper, these letters are not accessible to potential supporters who don't have computers or e-mail accounts; therefore, the Surfriders also send appeal letters via "snail mail."

Most appeal letters are sponsored by some larger organization, such as a nonprofit agency, and therefore represent national or local public literacies. Sometimes, though, appeal letters take the form of everyday public literacies. Such letters might be published in a church newsletter, on flyers posted around town or tucked in mailboxes, or on e-mail (as with James and Chandler's efforts to promote their Yellow Bike program, discussed in Chapter 4). Everyday appeal letters are usually inspired by specific events rather than ongoing membership drives or fundraising efforts. Examples include documents requesting donations of household goods for a congregation member whose home was destroyed in a fire, contributions to Toys for Tots, or assistance in finding a lost pet.

The content and form of everyday appeal letters is fairly flexible. However, most organizations want to give the impression that their issue is so urgent that they don't have time to write formal letters. To achieve this goal, they often adapt standard business letter format in order to make their appeal letters appear hastily composed—for example, by using a comma after the greeting and closing, indenting paragraphs, omitting the date, and making liberal use of exclamation marks and ellipses (. . .). Appeal letters might further deviate from formal business letter conventions by printing photographs directly onto the page, using computer fonts that resemble handwriting, extending their message over several pages, and running their address across the bottom of the first page. Many add a "P.S." at the end.

Most organizations purchase mailing lists from other sources who share similar ideals or constituencies—veterans' advocacy groups, for example, might buy addresses from the American Association for Retired Persons (AARP), or vice versa. While this practice might assist groups in reaching a large and receptive audience, it can also have the opposite effect. Some people receive so many appeal letters that they can't distinguish one group's "urgent" needs from those of another; feeling overwhelmed, these potential members of a rhetorical audience may simply discard appeal letters without reading them.

The lesson here is that audiences for appeal letters should be chosen carefully. While you want to reach many people efficiently, you also want to ensure that your letter will actually be read. In general, readers are more receptive to letters that *appear* to be written to them personally, even if they know this isn't the case. If you received three appeal letters from organizations whose interests you shared, which would you be most inclined to read further: the one that begins "To Our Friends at 5310 Clear Run Drive," the one that begins "Dear American Patriot," or one that greets you by name?

Computer programs can assist you in customizing appeal letters sent to mass audiences. It's worth remembering, though, that some people regard appeal letters as the public literacy equivalent of telemarketing, and thus simply refuse to read them, regardless of how personal they appear. This constraint can make appeal letters a risky genre choice.

Because they are usually asking people to give support or even money, it is common for appeal letters to resort to extreme emotional tactics, including shocking pictures or stories, to demonstrate the urgency of their cause. These messages might even appear on the envelope, such as this one from an international children's advocacy organization:

HANDLE WITH CARE

HEAT & WATER

MAY CAUSE SEVERE

DAMAGE

URGENT: OPEN IMMEDIATELY

The envelope contained some complimentary cabbage seeds, and next to a picture of a severely malnourished child, the letter read, in part: "Hold the packet of seeds as you look at this little child—you are holding his life in your hands!!"

Although the organization's goals might be worthy and its letter's claims accurate, you should be critical of such tactics as a reader; and although they can be very effective, you should use them sparingly as a writer. If you ever work for a nonprofit agency or political party—as an employee or a volunteer—you may be asked to draft an appeal letter. While the use of emotionalism might be appropriate in such letters, it is essential that your information be completely accurate in order to maintain your own credibility and that of your organization.

Exercise

Collect several examples of national, local, and everyday appeal letters and examine them in small groups. What common features do they share? What, if anything, distinguishes one from another? How would you characterize the language and tone of the letters? After reading their letters, are you interested in supporting any of these organizations or efforts? Why or why not?

Open Letters

Open letters are typically placed by individuals or special interest groups in local or national publications for the purpose of invoking the support of a receptive audience. In most cases, they are used to clarify information; express apologies, explanations, disapproval, or gratitude; ask for support; or outline a political agenda.

Sometimes open letters take the form of editorials that are written by columnists for publication in local or national periodicals. Often, though, they are simply paid advertisements or public relations efforts that resemble personal letters, business memos, or news items. Such constraints tend to limit this genre—at least at the local and national levels—to professional writers and individuals or groups who can afford to buy advertising space. Even though open letters may address issues in the public interest, it is a good idea to read their claims critically, as you would a television commercial or political advertisement, for evidence of bias or self interest.

Even if they do not use traditional business letter format, many open letters—like the following one from Unidad Cubana—are published on the official letterhead of an office or organization (fig. 6.1). And while this letter doesn't include a formal greeting, closing, or actual signatures, it purposefully evokes these conventions. On the surface, the letter appears only to articulate its positions on various aspects of American foreign policy affecting Cuba. However, by publishing its letter in the *Washington Monthly*—whose readers include politicians, political staff members, and private citizens capable of influencing the actions of politicians—the organization is also soliciting the support and political advocacy of its audience.

Open letters that appear in everyday public spheres typically do not represent advertising. On a grocery store bulletin board, you might see a notice thanking area residents for helping find a lost cat. After a tornado, the national news featured a family who had painted a message on the roof of their home thanking clean-up crews for their assistance. Although not all everyday open letters express gratitude, their purposes are usually to maintain interpersonal relationships and reinforce community values, not promote a special interest.

OPEN LETTER TO THE PRESIDENT AND THE CONGRESS OF THE UNITED STATES

A STATEMENT BY UNIDAD CUBANA

*"There is a limit to the tears shed over the graves of the dead,
and that is the infinite love of the Country that is sworn over their dead bodies."* — *José Martí*

Unidad Cubana publicly reaffirms the position it has been stating since its foundation on July 12, 1991, at Miami's Dade County Auditorium, when nearly all of the organizations and umbrella groups of Cuban exiles agreed that the only solution to the Cuban crisis was to face up to and overthrow the Castro regime.
Therefore, in view of the confusion that some of the exile organizations have created by changing this stand, Unidad Cubana, made up of dozens of organizations, reaffirms:

1) That in Cuba nothing has changed to justify trying to alter or change the policy on which Unidad Cubana labored along with other organizations and with our Congressmen in Washington, D.C., for the passing of the Helms-Burton Act.

2) That Unidad Cubana expresses that, in essence, nothing has changed in Cuba after the Pope's visit, even though some of those who seek an "understanding" with the Communist tyranny claim otherwise in order to weaken the U.S. embargo and create a false notion about the nature of the Castro regime.

3) That we continue to wholeheartedly support our Members of Congress, Ileana Ros-Lehtinen, Lincoln Díaz-Balart, and Bob Menéndez, whom we consider our voices in Washington, D.C., and to whom, therefore, we offer all the cooperation they need and is within our means to continue their patriotic struggle.

4) That we do not accept a solution based on the so-called "socialist laws" whereby those who are responsible for the destruction inflicted upon Cuba would be allowed to remain in power.

5) That Unidad Cubana, as an umbrella organization consisting of many member groups, respects their respective points of view as long as none of these is based on a dialog or *detente* with the tyranny.

6) That, just as we shall continue to help the dissident groups and the independent press, as well as those patriots who are waging war on the regime inside Cuba, we shall also continue to mobilize internationally to denounce those who would take over the resources stolen from Cuban and foreign citizens. Once Cuba is free of Castroism, we shall take these unscrupulous usurpers to court and force them to pay the appropriate reparations for their collaboration with Castro's totalitarian regime.

7) That we urge all those who agree with the total liberation of Cuba, and with the indictment of the criminals, to add their signatures to this Statement and join Unidad Cubana to help accomplish its high goals. Please call us at (305) 649-6950.

8) The leaders of Unidad Cubana reiterate their commitment to our country, to the people inside Cuba, and to the Cubans in exile, in order to achieve what those who have died on the altar of the Fatherland, the political prisoners, and those who chose the bitter path of exile, have been fighting for over the best years of their lives.

9) The only *Magna Carta* recognized by Unidad Cubana is the Constitution of 1940, which contains all the democratic elements that are needed for the reconstruction of Cuba.

10) Unidad Cubana wishes to take advantage of this opportunity to express its disagreement with the recent policy announced by the President of the United States in regard to Cuba. We feel that the almost 40 years of the Castro regime's inflexible totalitarian policy is more than sufficient to demonstrate that Fidel Castro will not change this policy because the U.S. government allows humanitarian aid to Cuba or direct flights to that country. Among many other things that we could state is the fact that this weak policy of opening to Castro without Castro making a single move concerning the respect of human rights in Cuba or its democratization, shows the dictator that to obtain concessions from the United States what he has to do is to continue oppressing the Cuban people.

Signed in Miami, Florida, U.S.A., in March, 1998, and read in a room of the Congress of the United States before Members of Congress friendly to Cuba's freedom, and the leadership of the Unidad Cubana.

P.O. Box 1973 / Miami, FL 33135 • 807 S.W. 25 Ave. / Oficina 209 / Miami, FL 33135 • Telefonos: (305) 649-6950 • Fax: (305) 649-7054

Figure 6.1. Individuals or organizations must usually pay to publish open letters like this one, which appeared in *Washington Monthly*. Such documents may represent a form of advertising or public relations, and should be scrutinized carefully for possible conflicts of interest.[1]

There are, of course, exceptions and ambiguities. For example, a local hot dog vendor whose business permit was revoked for health violations erected a sandwich board near his establishment; labeled "An Open Letter to New Hanover County Commissioners," the document alleged a variety of unfair administrative practices. Whether the vendor's open letter was in the public interest or his own self interest is debatable, but his claims did reach a rhetorical audience who contacted the County Commissioners on his behalf.

The form of an open letter will be dictated primarily by the public sphere in which it appears. If you are paying for advertising space, you probably want your letter to be as correct and professional-looking as possible; you may wish to examine other examples of open letters as models or consult an advertising agent at your target publication. As a general rule, audiences are more willing to overlook editing errors if you are thanking or praising them for something, or if the document is clearly informal and expects nothing but goodwill from its audience.

The most important criteria for evaluating an open letter, or for deciding whether you should write one yourself, are whether it addresses an issue that is legitimately in the public interest, and which public sphere is most accessible to a rhetorical audience.

Exercise

Search an electronic database using the keyword "open letter." Although you can probably read the texts on-line, track down several of the citations at your campus or local library so that you can see the letters in their original form. Compare and contrast several examples. In general, what kinds of rhetorical situations do open letters respond to?

Look through your writer's notebook. Can you find any rhetorical situations for which an open letter might be an appropriate response?

Peer Review

Before writing a letter in the public interest, you should work through the "Thinking Rhetorically" checklists in Chapters 3 and 4 to make sure that this is an appropriate response to an urgent rhetorical situation. Before submitting your letter, you should ask someone you trust to read it with the following questions in mind:

*   What is the purpose of this letter? Does it clearly and concisely identify the problem and explain why the writer finds this situation urgent? Does it request a specific, feasible action?

*   Does the letter address or invoke an appropriate rhetorical audience? Is the writer's relationship to the recipient clearly specified or implied?

*   Is the letter respectful of the audience's intelligence and values? Does it include accurate information, with a minimum of emotional appeals?

*   How would you characterize the language, tone, and style of the letter? Are these appropriate to the letter's audience and purpose?

*   In the case of letters to the editor, does the draft conform to the editorial guidelines described in the target publication?

*   In the case of other letters, does the draft conform to or appropriately modify standard business letter format?

- In the case of appeal letters, does the draft identify its sponsor? Does the sponsoring individual or group sound credible?

- After reading the letter, are you inclined to accept the writer's perspective or take the action he/she proposes? Why or why not?

- Is there anything in the letter that strikes you as especially wrong, uninformed, inappropriate, offensive, or suspect? If so, what?

- If there are any problems, how might they be addressed in a revision?

Note

1. *Washington Monthly.* May 1998: 45.

CHAPTER 7

Focus on Press Releases, Press Conferences, and Press Kits

Working with the media is an inevitable part of public literacy. And while the idea of publicity might seem more common among professional marketers, politicians, or celebrities—people promoting a new product or trying to get elected to office—it can also be used by non-professionals to persuade audiences that a rhetorical situation is urgent and demands their immediate action.

Writing press releases, compiling press kits, and holding press conferences all represent ways to facilitate media coverage of an event; they allow you or your group to create your own news story that represents *your* perspective and *your* agenda. As the word *press* implies, these genres are designed to address the media. However, you can also compile public information kits to inform and influence the actions of other audiences. This chapter will address each of these genres in turn, offering general guidelines about when they are appropriate and how to write them effectively.

Press Releases

The basic purpose of a *press release* is to announce something—an event, the results of a study, a major accomplishment or undertaking—in a way that attracts positive public attention, or publicity. The press releases you are most likely to write are those that respond to a lack of media attention to an issue in the public interest. In such cases, press releases can actually "create" news by invoking an audience who cares about what you have to say. When the mainstream local newspaper in Wilmington did not report allegations of racial imbalances among county school teachers, for example, concerned citizens might have been able to publicize the information through a press release.

Writing a press release allows you to control the telling of your story, which can be especially important when announcing bad news. Most media outlets welcome well-written press releases, and may even read or publish them verbatim. If this happens, then your press release has been successful. However, if *you* can reap the benefits of a cooperative media, then so can individuals or groups that are *not* acting in the public interest. It's important, therefore, to think critically about what the media publishes as news—that is, to consider who wrote it and whose interests it represents.

As with any rhetorical situation, your press release must address or invoke an audience who can act on your document. Since the first goal is to get your press release published, the most important rhetorical audience is initially the gatekeeper: the person who reads the press release and decides whether to reject it or accept it, and thus whether to make it accessible to a wider public. Understanding local knowledge can help you to anticipate the biases or interests of specific gatekeepers, as well as the kinds of issues that local public audiences tend to respond to.

Media outlets receive many press releases every day. Therefore the format and style of your press release can be as important as the content. Although these conventions vary slightly, adhering to them will enhance your credibility and increase the likelihood that your release will get careful consideration.

Your first step is to design press release *letterhead* for your organization or concern: stationery that includes the name or logo of your group, as well as its address and phone number, followed by the words "Press Release" or "Media Release." (Both legal and letter-sized paper are appropriate for letterhead.) You should send your press releases in envelopes matching the press release letterhead in style, ink color, and paper color; especially urgent press releases may also be sent by fax or e-mail.

At the left of your release, underneath the letterhead, you should type "For Release: Immediate" or "For Release: [Date]." If you don't want the information released until a specific date and time, type "Embargoed for Release Until [Date and Time]." Directly across from this information, type "Contact:" and then the name and phone number of the person who can answer questions about the information (usually the person who writes the release).

The content of press releases is generally single-spaced, with double spaces between paragraphs. The basic format of a press release includes these features:

> *Slug*: the title or headline typed in all capital letters and/or bold; should briefly summarize the content of the release, using action verbs to sound as interesting and newsworthy as possible
>
> *Lead*: the first paragraph (1–2 sentences); should answer who, what, when, where, and why, as well as so what? and who cares?
>
> *Body*: should adhere to an "inverted triangle" style, in which the most important information appears first, then slightly less important information, and so on; time constraints may force editors to read only the first few lines of press releases

before making a decision whether to use them, so it's important that all necessary information be immediately accessible

The style of a press release should be short, succinct, and specific; use exact names and dates whenever possible, and make sure your information is completely accurate. Press releases should communicate factual information; they are not editorials. Therefore opinions should either be conveyed through documented quotes or omitted altogether.

Releases should rarely go over one page, but in the rare instances that they do, type "(more)" at the center bottom of any page that is not your last page. Centered at the bottom of the last page, type "###" or "-30-" to indicate the end of the release (fig. 7.1). (Both symbols are acceptable but "-30-" is somewhat outdated.)

ODA Committee

PRESS RELEASE

Ontario Association of the Deaf (OAD)

December 14, 1998

**Premier Harris has SCROOGED Bill 83 -
Ontarians with Disabilities Act**

Monday, December 14, 1998: For Immediate Release

On December 15th, 1998 at 7 p.m. at the Bob Rumball Centre for the Deaf on 2395 Bayview St. The Ontario Association of the Deaf (OAD) is hosting the Emergency Community Forum to demand that the Harris Government withdraw and replace Bill 83 with a strong, effective and enforceable Ontarians with Disabilities Act now.

"This proposed legislation clearly violates the Supreme Court of Canada's landmark ruling in the Eldridge vs British Columbia case" says **Chris Kenopic**, President, Ontario Association of the Deaf. "Bill 83 is useless and an insult to our Deaf consumers."

David Lepofsky, co-chair of the ODA Committee and **Gary Malkowski**, former MPP York East are invited to speak at the Community Forum.

On November 23, 1998, Minister of Citizenship, **Isabel Bassett** introduced Bill 83, the Ontarians with Disabilities Act into the legislature, claiming that this Bill represents the fulfilment of Premier Harris 1995 election promise to introduce an ODA within his first term of office.

The Ontario Association of the Deaf joins the ODA Committee, a voluntary coalition of individuals and organizations concerned with the rights of people with disabilities in asking Premier Harris to withdraw Bill 83 and replace it with a strong and meaningful ODA.

For more information, contact **Chris Kenopic** at:
(416) 513-1893 TTY
(416) 413-822 Fax

- 30 -

Figure 7.1. This press release illustrates several minor modifications of conventional press release format.

Most press releases are directed to national or local publics, specifically, media outlets and their audiences. But it's also possible to use writing to release information to everyday publics (fig. 7.2). If, for example, you wanted to remind your neighbors to attend the annual block party, you might distribute flyers in mailboxes; if you wanted to announce the winners of your dormitory's elections, you might write an informal press release for the hall newsletter, or simply create a congratulatory poster. In such situations, "press" release might be something of a misnomer, since the announcements are not mediated by a gatekeeper or other member of the media.

Exercise

In your writer's notebook, make a list of projects you are currently involved in and significant developments in your life. This list might include a research paper you're working on, an upcoming trip, a new relationship . . . anything at all that's interesting or important to you. Then, choose one item from your list and write a press release announcing it. Remember, many press releases are designed to promote "soft news" that the media would not otherwise cover, so you need to make them sound as urgent as possible, and attend carefully to format and style conventions.

WESTWOOD

Neighborhood

NEWS

Notice of Public Hearing

Your comments are invited on the proposed...

Westwood/Highland Park Neighborhood Plan

and the Mayor's Proposed Response to the Plan

The Seattle City Council will hold a presentation and public hearing

Thursday, June 10, 1999
Presentation: 6:00 p.m. - Public Hearing: 7:00 p.m.
Highland Park United Methodist Church
Fellowship Hall
9001 9th Ave SW (entrance on 10th Ave)

Information about the plan and a sign-up sheet for those wishing to testify will be available at 6:00 p.m.

The proposed Westwood/Highland Park Neighborhood Plan was developed by citizen volunteers working together to enhance and preserve existing natural resources, strengthen connections between the community, preserve existing single family areas, improve multi-family areas, improve transportation and strengthen the neighborhood's economic core. The Mayor's proposed response includes:

- a resolution recognizing the plan and approving a work program for the City to begin implementing portions of the plan; and
- an ordinance with amendments to the City of Seattle's 20-year Comprehensive Plan and amendments to the Seattle Land Use Code.

Figure 7.2. This press release was published in a neighborhood newsletter. As an everyday public literacy document, it is less constrained by conventions regulating format and style.

Press Kits

The basic purpose of a *press kit* is to help the media cover an event or news story. The more information journalists have at their fingertips, the less work they will have to do in terms of double-checking facts, interviewing sources, and so on, and the more likely they will be to give favorable media coverage to a matter you or your group finds urgent. As with press releases, the most important audience for a press kit is the member of the media who sees it and decides whether the information is newsworthy. A good press kit should make the gatekeeper's decision as easy as possible.

Press kits are helpful when a rhetorical situation is complicated or involves several parties—that is, when there are multiple opportunities for confusion, such as misspelling names or misunderstanding key information. Let's say, for example, that you are holding a press conference to announce the results of a study jointly sponsored by three organizations for the purpose of documenting wheelchair access to public buildings in your community. A press kit might include a press release announcing the results of the study, a copy of the study itself, informational brochures related to the sponsoring agencies, and copies of any laws or ordinances related to disability access.

The simplest press kit assembles a press release and a few other documents, called attachments, in a pocketed "presentation folder," which may feature a group's name or logo. Common examples of attachments include the following:

"backgrounders" or fact sheets	mission or policy statements
FAQ (frequently asked questions) sheets	calendars or schedules of events
copies of relevant studies or press coverage	budgets and timetables
photographs (with captions) or videotapes	maps or floor plans
list of photo or interview opportunities	promotional flyers or brochures
biographical sketches of people mentioned prominently in press release	

Of course, too much information can overwhelm an audience, so you probably won't include all of these items in your press kit. Likewise, you can probably think of many other documents that could be appropriate. The choice of attachments depends on your goals and the rhetorical situation.

You may decide to include in your press kit documents compiled or appropriated from other sources (e.g., newspaper clippings, information sheets). This is generally acceptable as long as you document your sources (somebody researched and wrote each of those documents, after all) and include an adequate number of attachments that were prepared specifically in response to this rhetorical situation. As with all public documents, your press kit needs to convey the urgency of the rhetorical situation; if it includes too much "recycled" material, the event or information you are announcing may seem stale—hence not newsworthy.

When arranging a press kit in a presentation folder, always place the two most important documents at the front of the pocket on each side of the folder; one of these is usually the press release. Arrange additional documents behind these, in the order in which you want your audience to see them. You might want to attach a cover letter to the front of the folder describing the contents of the press kit and, if applicable, an agenda for the press conference.

The presentation of your press kits is constrained primarily by its purpose and content, but also by your budget. If you were promoting soft news, such as a beach carnival to raise money for Special Olympics, you might put the contents of your press kit in a plastic bucket or include a carnival token. This kind of packaging wouldn't detract from the message, and might even enhance it. If, on the other hand, you were attempting to draw attention to diminished water quality in area streams, "gimmicky" packaging might undermine the seriousness of your announcement and thus would not be appropriate. Instead, you would probably use a plain or specially designed folder or binding, and include more straightforward, informational documents.

Public Information Kits

Press kits are generally distributed to members of the print and broadcast media in the context of an important news announcement. Individuals or groups might also give supporters *public information kits* or "tool kits" to encourage informed action. Every summer, for example, Wilmington, North Carolina, sponsors a "Hurricane Expo" and distributes public information kits that include a hurricane tracking map, a map of evacuation routes and shelters, a checklist of preparation tips, and emergency phone numbers. Political candidates may also prepare public information kits for potential supporters.

Because press kits and public information kits differ in both audience and purpose, they often contain different information. For example, while press kits almost always include a press release, public information kits almost never do. Public information kits may include the following attachments:

an appeal letter	biographical sketches
mission or policy statements	FAQ sheets
buttons, bumper stickers, or decals	calendar of events
membership information and applications	sample letters of concern
contact information for elected officials	volunteer opportunities
coupons or discount offers from supportive businesses	

Public information kits usually go directly to a rhetorical audience rather than through a gatekeeper. Thus they are constrained by fewer conventions regarding format and style. As always, the content and presentation of a public information kit must be appropriate for its purpose and audience.

James and Chandler prepared a public information kit to distribute to students and staff at the back-to-school activities fair in an effort to generate interest in SCAT, the Yellow Bike program, and alternative transportation methods in general. Worried that presentation folders would appear too serious and that students might throw them away without even looking at the contents, James and Chandler persuaded SCAT to allocate money for the purchase of inexpensive water bottles printed with the SCAT logo. They then stuffed these bottles with information about their organization, including a calendar of events and contact person, a bike registration form, a coupon for a free bike tune-up, and a shuttle schedule.

Exercise

In your writer's notebook, make a list of organizations you belong to or are interested in joining; add to that list names of any individuals or groups you can think of who are involved in some interesting project (e.g., a political campaign, a dog walk-a-thon). Choose one individual or group from your list and schedule an appointment to talk to them about their interests, goals, and any upcoming events they will be involved in. Collect any written documents the person or group has designed for their own use or to promote their projects or concerns.

Once you've done this initial research, design a press or public information kit for the individual or group: decide what attachments would inform a rhetorical audience and persuade them to act, what kind of presentation would be appropriate, and why. A campus group whose primary goals are social might have different needs than one whose purposes are more service-oriented; likewise, community groups might have different needs than student groups. If you feel committed to the person or group you profile, you might want to create the press or public information kit for their use.

Peer Review

Before writing a press release or preparing a press or public information kit, you should work through the "Thinking Rhetorically" checklists in Chapters 3 and 4 to make sure these are appropriate responses to an urgent rhetorical situation. Before submitting your documents to a suitable audience, ask someone you trust to read it with the following questions in mind:

- Is it clear why the rhetorical situation to which this document responds is urgent for a public audience?

- What action(s) does this document call for? Does the document give the audience enough information to take those actions easily and effectively?

- How would you characterize the language, tone, style, and presentation of the document(s)? Are these appropriate to the audience and purpose?

- Do the documents conform to style and format conventions for press releases and press or public information kits?

- Do any documents strike you as irrelevant or inappropriate? If so, why?

- After reading the document(s), are you inclined to take the actions the writer proposes? Why or why not?

- If there are any problems, how might they be addressed in a revision?

Press Conferences

Press conferences provide opportunities for media interaction with your news in the form of photo opportunities, question and answer sessions, or other experiences. For example, at the end of a press conference announcing a coral reef research project, a group of scientists invited members of the media to scuba dive down to its undersea laboratory. Press conferences are usually accompanied by press kits and press releases, and should be reserved for very significant announcements. If an organization calls press conferences too often, the media won't be able to distinguish the urgent news from the merely routine announcement and may stop paying attention.

The anatomy of a press conference works something like this:

1. Determine the importance of the news.
   - Is it urgent?
   - How can its urgency be conveyed to the media?

2. Set up the press conference.
   - How should the press conference be announced (e.g., by phone, fax, regular mail, or e-mail)?
   - Who should serve as the spokesperson?
   - What should we say?
   - What time and location are appropriate to the message?

3. Create appropriate documents. These may include:

    • Press release and/or press kits for members of the media

    • "Talking points" or remarks for spokesperson(s)

    • Agenda

4. Structure the press conference. Typical features include:

    • Welcome to media and guests

    • Description of the contents of the press kit, if any

    • Introduction of the spokesperson

    • Remarks

    • Formal question and answer period

    • Photo and interview opportunities (e.g., media outlets talk to speaker for sound bites)

As with press kits, gimmicks within press conferences are only appropriate to promote soft news. For example, when one university recently installed baby changing stations in its sports complex, they held a press conference in the men's bathroom.

Although some press conferences might be lively and informal, nothing you do or say in that setting is "off the record." In other words, it's important to behave professionally at all times: anticipate logistical complications and stay in control. It goes without saying, furthermore, that spokespersons should speak clearly and dress appropriately for the event; usually this means conservative clothing.

Exercise

Call the public information office for your school or local government, and ask if there is an upcoming press conference you can attend. If possible, go to the press conference and in your writer's notebook, take notes on how the spokesperson(s) organize and orchestrate the event. What do they wear? How do they speak and behave? How do they handle logistical details such as scheduling, seating, late arrivals, noise, or interruptions? In your opinion, are the details of the press conference appropriate to the rhetorical situation?

CHAPTER 8

Focus on Grant Proposals

If you've ever applied for a scholarship or other money to help defray the costs of going to college, then you've applied for a grant. While these kinds of grants aren't exactly in the public interest (except in the sense that an educated citizenry is in the public interest), the application process is similar to the requests for financial support that are submitted by schools, nonprofit organizations, and other individuals and groups every day. Each of these groups is trying to persuade an audience to give them money for some worthy project.

Although grant money is widely available, grant proposals are among the most complicated genres of public writing, and competition for funding can be fierce. For these reasons, skilled grant writers are highly sought after by groups and institutions working in the public interest. Grants are usually awarded to organized institutions, many of which employ professional grant writers. Nevertheless, grant money is also accessible to everyday citizens who come together to solve problems. This chapter will discuss how to use writing to locate and take advantage of grant opportunities.

Finding the Right Funding Opportunities

National, local, and everyday public spheres offer a variety of grant opportunities (fig. 8.1). They range from the very large (millions of dollars, often to support extensive projects with several participants and disbursed over several years) to the very small (as little as $500 or less). The Ben & Jerry's Foundation, for example, offers grants to nonprofit groups throughout the United States for projects that meet the Foundation's criteria. Although it primarily offers "full grants" ($1001–$15,000), it also considers applications for "small grants" (up to $1000) "for innovative programs that fit into our general guidelines and that are infused with a spirit of hopefulness."

The Ben & Jerry's Foundation also distributes small grants to "Community Action Teams" within its home state of Vermont, and indeed, many granting institutions prefer to fund projects that have a direct and positive impact on a local—that is, geographically specific—public sphere. Families, civic groups, and local businesses often establish charitable foundations to benefit the residents of their community. The Cooper Foundation in Waco, Texas, for example, describes its mission as "mak[ing] Waco a better or more desirable city in which to live." Because of these very local goals, the Foundation offers grants "exclusively to nonprofit organizations in the Waco area."

Everyday grant opportunities are probably the most difficult to find, because they generally exist "off the radar." They are available informally through private donors or unincorporated groups (e.g., neighborhood associations) rather than through nonprofit agencies and philanthropic institutions. Everyday grants generally aren't advertised; in fact, individuals or groups who are willing to fund projects in the public interest might not even plan to do so until they are approached with a promising idea. If this is one of the constraints you are facing as you apply for a grant, you might have to work harder to demonstrate the urgency of the problem you are addressing and the feasibility of the solution you are proposing.

Special Activity Fund Guidelines

The purpose of the Special Activity Fund is to support educational and student centered programs and activities. Priority is given to projects and events that are open to the entire campus community. Further priority is given to organizations that have attempted their own fundraising. Any person or group requesting funds must be prepared to demonstrate how the UNCW campus will benefit from the project.

Organizations must complete the following two steps in order to request funds:

1. **Schedule a Time to Present your Request to the Appropriations Committee.**
   In order to request Special Activity Funds, student organizations must schedule a time to present their request to the Appropriations Committee. Presentations generally take ten to fifteen minutes and give the committee a comprehensive breakdown of the total project including the anticipated cost along with the purpose and scope of the event. **Please type all additional material and bring enough copies for 15 committee members.**

2. **Prepare for your Appropriations Committee Presentation**
   Please complete the following application and return it to the SGA Treasurer by the Monday preceding your presentation. Include all information and documentation that pertains to the funding request including your current budget (including expenses and revenue), conference or event paperwork, order forms, or registration materials.

> **For best consideration by the Appropriations Committee, please submit all requests at least three weeks prior to the event or project date. Please note, all Appropriation Committee recommendations must go before the SGA Senate for approval. Special Activity Fund Requests are not final until the SGA Senate makes a formal vote.**

Funding Guidelines

Travel	Equipment	Programming
• SGA will only fund up to four (4) people going on a trip	• All organizations must log their equipment with the SGA Business Manager annually	• Priority is given to events that are open to the entire campus community
• SGA will fund up to $85 per person for registration	• The president is responsible for the upkeep and care of the equipment	• Organizations must print "funded by the SGA" on all promotional materials for the event
• SGA will fund up to $43 per person per night	• Negligence will result in confiscation of equipment	
• SGA will fund $0.23/mile up to 400 miles	• All property is state property (must adhere to university guidelines)	• A list of all co-sponsors must accompany the Special Activity Fund request to the Appropriations Committee
• Food will not be covered		

Figure 8.1a. The Student Government Association at the University of North Carolina at Wilmington offers grants to support student-initiated projects and events through its Special Activity Fund. It is limited to, and designed to benefit, members of a geographically specific public sphere, and thus represents an example of local public literacy.

Special Activity Fund Request

_____
(Date Submitted)

_____
(Name of Organization)   (Number of Members)

_____
(Contact Person)   (Phone)

_____
(Date of Presentation)   (Time of Presentation)

Request for: ☐ Travel   ☐ Equipment   ☐ Programming   ☐ Other

Please Describe the Purpose of the Request: _____

_____
_____
_____
_____
_____
_____
_____
_____
_____
_____
_____
_____

Please List Any Co-Sponsors: _____

_____

Please List the Anticipated Revenue: _____

_____

Total Cost: _____

> All Special Activity request must be accompanied by supporting documentation
> in order to be considered by the Appropriations Committee.
> Please see the reverse side of this form for details to be provided.
> Please type all additional materials and bring fifteen copies of each
> to your presentation.

Figure 8.1b.

Some forms of everyday grant support are even more informal. If you ask your parents to help pay your college expenses, for example, you might agree to certain conditions and even put the terms of the support (e.g., maintaining a minimum GPA) into a written contract. Such requests can also be made in the public interest. For example, you might write a note to your landlord asking him to waive the normal rental fee for your apartment complex's conference facilities so that a service organization that you belong to can hold meetings there.

Supporting Documentation

Please provide the following information, typed, on a separate sheet of paper:
(see inside for guidelines)

For Travel Requests:

1. Destination
2. Lodging arrangements / Cost
3. Transportation / Cost
4. Registration / Cost
5. Number of people traveling
6. Amount fundraised by group
7. Total cost of travel
8. Total amount requested

For Programming Requests:

1. Date of event
2. Location
3. Cost of Admission (if charging)
4. Amount fundraised by group
5. Total cost of program
6. Total amount requested

For Equipment Requests:

1. Cost of equipment
2. Vendor
3. Include at least two other estimates for goods
4. Amount fundraised by group
5. Storage / Maintenance Plan
6. Total cost of equipment
7. Total amount requested

For All Other Requests:

1. Present a detailed account of request
2. Include estimates
3. Total amount of item or project
4. Total amount requested

**Please remember to contact the SGA Treasurer
to schedule a presentation for your organization to
the Appropriantions Committee
962-3553.**

Figure 8.1c.

Grant opportunities are frequently announced in newspapers and newsletters, and on flyers and websites, through "requests for proposals," or *RFPs*. At the library, you can find directories of such opportunities through the subject headings *grants-in-aid, block grants, fundraising,* and *charitable contributions*. On-line, you can do a search using the term *small grants* or check out the "Grantmaster" site at grantmaster.com/links.html.

If you are interested in a specific issue, such as disability rights, AIDS, or recycling, you can go directly to Websites or advocacy magazines that are concerned with these issues, such as *POZ* or *The Able Informer*, many of which announce RFPs. Most universities also have research offices which match faculty and students with appropriate funding sources, assist them in applying for grants, and sponsor grant-writing workshops.

Like other genres of public writing, grants respond to urgent rhetorical situations: problems that have potential solutions but no money to implement them. Such situations are perhaps most frequently encountered by nonprofit organizations, which derive their resources from donations, grants, and bequests, and thus work with limited and often unpredictable budgets.

When writing an appeal letter (see Chapter 6), your rhetorical audience is composed of individual *donors*. When writing a grant proposal, your rhetorical audience consists primarily of *funders*, or granting institutions, that might be willing to provide financial support for your project. As with many other public genres, grant proposals go first to gatekeepers—in this case, reviewers who read all grant proposals and decide which ones are in the public interest. "Public interest" is defined differently by different institutions, so when you are considering possible grant opportunities, look for consistency between the purpose and goals of your project and those of the granting institution. Although you will likely find several RFPs that seem well suited for your project, you might have to adapt your project description to meet grant criteria.

Exercise

Look through your writer's notebook for recurring interests, themes, or problems. Then, using the search strategies described above, locate several granting sources and RFPs that might be appropriate for supporting projects related to those issues. (For example, if you are concerned about domestic violence, then look for RFPs that share these concerns.) If you find the RFP on-line, print it out; if you find it in a book or periodical, write a letter requesting application guidelines and other available information.

Applying for a Grant: Three Steps

I. Preparation

Before you even start looking for a grant, you should do some preliminary writing to define your project's *goals* (what you want to accomplish) and *objectives* (how you will accomplish them). For example, SCAT's central goal was to expand transportation alternatives on campus and in their local community, and their initial objectives were to obtain and refurbish bikes for the Yellow Bike program. It's also a good idea at this stage to identify who will benefit from your project (both directly and indirectly) and how you will evaluate the success of your project.

Once you've outlined the basic purposes of your project, you can search for funders who share your priorities. Your first step after locating potential grant opportunities is to contact the funders and acquire applications and proposal guidelines, which include information about eligibility, submission deadlines, format requirements, and the proposal evaluation process. If possible, obtain a list of projects that the granting institution has supported in the past; this can give you an idea of whether your proposal has a good chance of being successful.

Grant guidelines and applications offer many clues as to what granting institutions value: current program interests, funding priorities, evaluation criteria, and so on. This information should suggest intellectual themes for your proposal, and may even provide a vocabulary for articulating exactly how your proposal matches the interests of the funder. Although it is often possible to propose the same project to several funders, submission policies and evaluation criteria vary widely even among grants with similar priorities. Be prepared to modify your proposal to meet the requirements of each grant.

National and local granting institutions generally do not award grants to individuals working independently in the public interest. Instead, they prefer to support projects undertaken by organized groups with an established identity, mission, and track record. Some applications may limit funding to nonprofit agencies, in which case applicants may have to provide documentation for their "501(c)(3) status" (see Chapter 4), including financial reports, a list of members of the Board of Directors, and so on.

2. Writing the Proposal

Most funders offer detailed guidelines on how to apply for grants. You should read these carefully for specifications regarding content, length, format, and other requirements. Ben & Jerry's, for example, states that application letters and proposals "should employ a readable font size (no less than 10 pt.) and one inch margins." The Bright Ideas educational grant, sponsored by the North Carolina Electric Membership Corporation, emphasizes that "Faxed applications will NOT be accepted."

It's not uncommon for you to run across RFPs that simply request you to "submit a proposal." Luckily, grant proposals include several standard features that you can use and adapt even if the granting agency doesn't provide more thorough guidelines. These features include the following:

> *Statement of need*: purpose and goals of project, measurable objectives, and compelling reasons why the proposal should be supported; background on the problem your project is designed to improve

- Use a funnel approach: start with the generalized problem as it occurs in your community and move to the conditions which make this a problem.

- Describe current resources that address the problem, identify gaps in those resources, and explain how your proposal will fill these gaps.

- Prepare to do whatever research is necessary to offer evidence of the need for the program and the appropriateness and feasibility of your solution.

Plan: method and process of accomplishing goals and objectives

- Specify actions or measures you will take to achieve your goals.

- Describe personnel qualifications (including volunteers).

- Tailor the description of the project to the interests, priorities, and goals of the funding source.

Evaluation: how you will know whether you are meeting your goals

- Describe plans for record keeping and assessment of data.

- Identify measurable milestones that you will reach along the way.

Project timeline: start and finish dates; schedule of activities

Credentials: information about the applicant and organization that verifies your ability to successfully undertake project, including history and mission of organization, population served, and previous accomplishments

Budget: cost projections

- Don't round out numbers; use bids and estimates when possible.

- Don't pad: if reviewers suspect that you are deceiving them on budget projections, they might mistrust other parts of your application.

- Include all sources of support, including volunteer time, donations, and so on.

Supporting materials: additional information requested as part of your application (e.g., letters of reference, resumes)

Proposals are typically written in narrative form, with the categories listed above (or other categories specified by the guidelines) functioning as subheadings to enhance the readability of your document. You should double space between paragraphs and subsections of the narrative, and you may wish to format your proposal in block style. (This textbook makes use of both of these formatting conventions; see also Chapter 6.) The content and form of a grant can be adapted to meet the needs of different rhetorical situations—for example, proposing a project at school or at your workplace for which you need guidance or time off, but no money.

The easiest thing to remember when applying for a grant is also one of the most important: *follow instructions*. Most grant reviewers appreciate concise proposals that they can read and understand quickly. So if the guidelines request a one-page letter, don't send a two-page letter. If the application requires you to enclose several items with your proposal, make yourself a checklist and include all of them. If there is a submission deadline, mark it on your calendar and allow yourself plenty of time to meet it (including time to get necessary signatures and mail your materials). Failure to follow directions won't necessarily mean that your proposal will be rejected or ignored, but why take chances?

3. Follow-Up

Funding organizations usually inform applicants once they have received your materials. If you don't hear from them, it's appropriate to contact them about the status of your proposal.

Eventually you will be notified whether or not the funder has chosen to support your project. If your proposal was unsuccessful, don't give up. Most grant reviewers are willing to provide feedback about a proposal's strengths and weaknesses, and this information can help you to revise your proposal for resubmission. Agencies that receive a large volume of submissions might not be available to provide extensive feedback, in which case you might want to consult a more experienced grant writer for guidance. The research office at your university might provide this service at no charge.

If your proposal was successful, write a thank you letter to the funder immediately. If you are expected to submit written reports or other materials documenting the success of your project, take these responsibilities seriously. Since many grants are renewable, it's important to let funders know that they made the right decision in supporting your project.

Regardless of whether your project receives support, it's important to maintain productive, professional relationships with granting agencies. This is especially true in local and everyday public spheres, where funders may also be neighbors or peers—and where the beneficiaries of your project are likely not only to know you personally, but to depend on you to work in their interest. Money introduces a variety of constraints into the rhetorical situation, which public writers must anticipate and appropriately address.

Peer Review

As always, you should work through the "Thinking Rhetorically" checklists in Chapters 3 and 4 before undertaking a grant proposal. Before submitting your proposal to a funder, provide a copy of the submission guidelines to someone you trust and ask that person to read both the guidelines and your proposal carefully with these questions in mind:

- What is the purpose of this proposal? Does it clearly and concisely identify the problem and explain why the writer finds this situation urgent? Does it propose a specific, feasible action?

- Is the proposal addressed to an appropriate rhetorical audience? Does it meet the eligibility criteria of the grant (if any)? Is the proposed project consistent with the interests of the funding source?

- Does the application and/or proposal include all required information and materials?

- Does it echo the language and intellectual themes of the grant? Does it clearly align the project with the interests, goals, and priorities of the funding source?

- Does it conform to the style, format, and length specifications (if any) described in the grant guidelines? Does it employ features that enhance readability?

- How would you characterize the language, tone, and style of the application/proposal? Are these appropriate to the document's audience and purpose?

- After reading the application/proposal, are you persuaded that this project deserves funding? Why or why not?

- Is there anything in the application or proposal that would benefit from additional research? If so, what?

- If there are any problems, how might they be addressed in a revision?

Grant Writing in Action

Tracy's investigations into local knowledge (see Chapter 5) inspired her to create a "newspapers in education" program in the local schools using the *Wilmington Journal*, a weekly newspaper with a primarily African American audience. (The local daily newspaper, the *Wilmington Morning Star*, has already established such a program.) After researching subscription costs and confirming that none of the local public school libraries carry the *Journal*, Tracy drafted the following description of her goals and objectives:

Project Goals

improve literacy among local African American students

expose them to news, information, and voices from the local black community

enrich the literacy environment in African American homes

promote cultural diversity by exposing all students and faculty to different perspectives on local news

encourage schools to expand their reading material

increase political participation among African American residents

<u>Objectives</u>

obtain *Journal* subscriptions for libraries at all local public schools

offer subscriptions at reduced rates for students and staff

create study guides for each issue (ways to use newspaper in different classes)

organize study groups to discuss each issue

As she looked at her lists, Tracy realized that she would need help implementing her plan. Although she was fairly certain that members of various student groups—such as the English Club or Student Education Association—might be willing to run the project as volunteers, the study guides would probably have to be prepared by teachers. She therefore updated her budget plan to include teacher stipends and photocopying expenses as well as subscriptions to the *Journal*.

In her writer's notebook, Tracy recorded questions, resources, and potential constraints related to her project—issues she would have to reconsider or research further before addressing them in her grant application. These issues included:

African American population in county; in local public schools

test scores for African American students

percentage of African American clients at Cape Fear Literacy Council

national statistics on illiteracy?

voter turnout in recent elections—Board of Elections (are statistics available according to race?)

circulation for *Journal* and *Morning Star*—statistics on readership by race, age, etc.

literacy practices in African American homes (find textbooks for "Politics of Literacy" class)

information on *Morning Star* "newspaper in education" program—prices, support for teachers, benefits

how to evaluate program?? surveys?

how would newspapers be delivered?

who will help me??

As she reflected on her list of questions and potential obstacles, Tracy scaled down her project's objectives: to provide annual subscriptions of the *Journal* to all local public schools, to subsidize annual subscriptions for all interested students and teachers, and to schedule weekly discussion groups at high schools and community centers. After talking to teachers at local high schools, she also reluctantly gave up her plan to create study guides or hire teachers to do so, since reading each issue of the newspaper and creating worthwhile lesson ideas to accompany them would have to be done on a weekly basis. Before committing to such a rigorous schedule (and asking others to do the same) Tracy decided first to explore the level of local interest in reading the *Journal*.

Tracy's next step was to locate suitable grant opportunities, which she did by searching the Internet using the phrase *education grants*. However, she quickly discovered that such grants were either too big for her modest project (hundreds of thousands of dollars or more, designed to implement large-scale curricular changes) or limited to professional teachers or administrators.

Using the term *small grants*, Tracy eventually located several promising RFPs, and eventually narrowed her selections down to the Bradley Foundation, which supports projects that "seek to reinvigorate and reempower the traditional, local institutions—families, schools, churches, and neighborhoods—that provide training in and room for the exercise of genuine citizenship." After carefully reading the Foundation's guidelines, which appear on the following pages (fig. 8.2a, 8.2b, and 8.2c), Tracy made a detailed list of funding priorities, submission requirements, evaluation criteria, and important themes and phrases to incorporate into her proposal.

Tracy's search for grant opportunities revealed yet another obstacle: that most grants are limited to nonprofit organizations. So she made a list of local groups or agencies that might be willing to sponsor her project:

NAACP
Cape Fear Literacy Council
Parent-Teacher Organizations
1898 Reconciliation Foundation

Since she already had an interest in working with community literacy programs professionally, Tracy chose to approach the Literacy Council first. The director of the agency was receptive to her idea, and agreed to provide feedback as Tracy drafted her proposal as well as to make available copies of the agency's mission statement and other necessary documents. The only condition was that Tracy not send the proposal until the agency had approved it, a condition to which Tracy readily consented.

Tracy adapted the standard proposal structure described earlier in this chapter to meet the specifications of the Bradley Foundation grant, which included the categories *Program Description*, *Project Personnel*, and *Sponsoring Institution or Agency*. What follows is the first draft of her program description that Tracy showed to the program coordinator at the Literacy Council:

The goals of the "*Wilmington Journal* Home-School Literacy Project" are to improve literacy performance among African American students; to enrich the

Current Program Interests

The Foundation's Board, on occasion, undertakes to define and redefine its current program interests. At present, the Foundation aims to encourage projects that focus on cultivating a renewed, healthier, and more vigorous sense of citizenship among the American people, and among peoples of other nations, as well.

The free society so central to the convictions and success of the Bradley brothers rests upon and is intended to nurture a solid foundation of competent, self-governing citizens, who are understood to be fully capable of and personally responsible for making the major political, economic, and moral decisions that shape their own lives, and the lives of their children. Such decisions are made on the basis of common sense, received wisdom, traditional values, and everyday moral understandings, which are in turn nurtured and passed on to future generations by healthy families, churches, neighborhoods, voluntary associations, schools, and other valuegenerabng "mediating structures."

This expansive understanding of citizenship is being challenged today, however, by contemporary forces and ideas that regard individuals more as passive and helpless victims of powerful external forces than as personally responsible, self-governing citizens, and that foster a deep skepticism about citizenly values and mediating structures. Consequently, authority and accountability tend to flow away from citizens toward centralized, bureaucratic, "service-providing" institutions which claim to be peculiarly equipped to cope with those external forces on behalf of their "clients." This systematic disenfranchisement of the citizen, and the consequent erosion of citizenly mediating structures, pose grave threats to the free society that the Bradley brothers cherished.

In light of these considerations, projects likely to be supported by the Foundation will generally share these assumptions:

- They will treat free men and women as genuinely self-governing, personally responsible citizens, not as victims or clients.
- They will aim to restore the intellectual and cultural legitimacy of citizenly common sense, the received wisdom of experience, everyday morality, and personal character, refurbishing their roles as reliable guideposts of everyday life.
- They will seek to reinvigorate and reempower the traditional, local institutions -- families, schools, churches, and neighborhoods -- that provide training in and room for the exercise of genuine citizenship, that pass on everyday morality to the next generation, and that cultivate personal character.
- They will encourage decentralization of power and accountability away from centralized, bureaucratic, national institutions back to the

Figure 8.2a. Application and proposal guidelines, such as these provided by the Bradley Foundation, provide information about what a granting agency values.

states, localities, and revitalized mediating structures where
citizenship is more fully realized.

In addition to these thematic considerations, eligible projects will exhibit
these features:

- They may address any arena of public life -- economics, politics,
  culture, or civil society -- where citizenship as here understood is an
  important issue. It is important to note that our view of citizenship is
  not primarily concerned with promoting civics education, voter
  awareness or turn-out, or similar activities narrowly focused on
  voting and elections.
- They may address the problem of citizenship at home or abroad,
  where the fall of many (and the perpetuation of some) totalitarian
  regimes has made this issue particularly urgent.
- In light of our emphasis on decentralization, and considering the
  Foundation's deep roots in Milwaukee and Wisconsin -- areas with
  proud traditions of innovation and experimentation in democratic
  citzenship -- community and state projects will be of particular
  interest to us. Such projects will aim to improve the life of the
  community through increasing cultural and educational
  opportunities, grass-roots economic development, and effective and
  humane social and health services, reflecting where possible the
  Foundation's focus on the resuscitation of citizenship.
- Projects may be actual demonstrations of the resuscitation of
  citizenship in the economic, political, cultural, or social realms;
  policy research and writing about approaches encouraging that
  resuscitation; academic research and writing that explore the
  intellectual roots of citizenship, its decline, and prospects for revival;
  and popular writing and media projects that illustrate for a broader
  public audience the themes of citizenship.

Much of the creative and energetic leadership essential for a renewal of
citizenship will be supplied by gifted individuals, who must receive
challenging and stimulating programs and instruction at all levels of their
education. The Foundation supports programs that research the needs of
gifted children and techniques of providing education for students with
superior skills and/or intelligence. Research programs investigating how
learning occurs in gifted children and demonstration programs of instruction
are to be considered.

Figure 8.2b.

APPLICATION PROCEDURE

Two steps are required in the application process. First, the applicant should prepare a brief letter of inquiry, describing the applicant's organization and intended project. If the Foundation determines the project to be within its current program interests the applicant will be invited to submit a formal proposal.

The second step is the actual submission of the proposal. Applicants should submit a letter presenting a concise description of the project, its objectives and significance, and the qualifications of the organizations and individuals involved. Included with the letter should be a project budget, the amount of the grant sought from The Bradley Foundation, and other sources of support. The applicant should complete the "Grantee Tax Exempt Status Information" form included with the Program Guidelines and submit a copy of the IRS letter confirming the organization's tax exempt and public support status under Sections 501(c)(3) and 509(a), respectively, of the Internal Revenue Code.

Meetings between the Foundation staff and applicants, where necessary, will be arranged after the receipt of a written proposal. Final authority for making grants rests with the Board of Directors, which meets four times a year, February, May/June, September, and November. The Directors act on grant requests after proposals have been comprehensively reviewed by Foundation staff. Each proposal is reviewed according to its unique characteristics. To be considered at one of these meetings, proposals should be submitted by the following dates: December 1, March 1, July 1, September 1.

Whenever possible, proposals submitted by these deadlines will be considered at the next Board meeting. However, circumstances may sometimes require a lengthier period of review.

Because of the necessarily limited resources of the Foundation, many worthwhile projects cannot be supported. The demands on the Foundation's resources also limit the size of particular grants and the ability of the Foundation to make commitments for extended periods.

Figure 8.2c.

literate environment in local homes; to promote cultural diversity by providing students and staff at local public schools with access to news and information written from African American perspectives; and to expand the reading materials offered at local schools.

The project will accomplish these goals by providing to schools, at no cost, annual subscriptions of the *Journal*, a weekly newspaper with a primarily African American readership and prominent advocacy role in the community, and offering subscriptions to individual students and staff at a reduced rate. Volunteers from the Cape Fear Literacy Center will lead weekly discussion sessions at schools and community centers to reinforce the content of the newspapers and apply it to other events and interests in the lives of the participants. Teachers will be made aware of the program and encouraged to make use of the newspaper in their lessons.

The project is inspired by research which shows that people become most proficient at reading and writing when the content and purpose of those skills are grounded in their lives. One assumption of the proposed project is that African American students and adults will find more reasons to write if they can see how language can help them to "name and claim" their lives.

Research also shows that people with strong interpersonal networks and feelings of cultural legitimacy are more likely to engage in civic behaviors. Thus a second assumption of this project is that African Americans—particularly the next generation of voters—will be inspired to take a more active role in civic affairs if they are provided with information on issues that are important to them and opportunities to discuss and act on that information.

The local daily newspaper, the *Wilmington Morning Star*, already sponsors a "newspapers in education" program, which is supported by subscribers who donate the cost of newspapers canceled when they go on vacation. That program is designed more for the study of current events and writing techniques rather than cultural diversity and civic enfranchisement. Because of a smaller circulation and limited budget, the *Journal* has never tried to create such a program. Therefore, the proposed project fills a gap in the community.

The project will run from September 1 to June 1 (the full academic year). Four times during this period, participants will fill out surveys documenting their literate and civic behaviors and attitudes, as well as their opinions about the program. These responses will be compiled to measure whether reading, discussing, and writing in response to the *Journal* has a measurable impact on the civic participation or attitudes of readers, specifically the feelings of intellectual and cultural legitimacy of African American citizens.

Consult the criteria for effective grant writing, the guidelines provided by the Bradley Foundation, and the peer review questions listed earlier in this chapter. Then reread Tracy's draft carefully. What suggestions would you offer her as she undertakes her revisions?

Exercise

With your writing group, brainstorm a list of problems on campus. Choose one problem, and brainstorm another list—this time, of projects that could improve or solve that problem. Then, using the guidelines for the SGA Special Activity Fund or a funding source at your own campus, write a one-paragraph description of the goals and objectives of your idea. Remember, grant reviewers appreciate writing that not only describes a project in clear, concise terms, but also explains how the project fits the specific interests and priorities of the funding institution.

CHAPTER 9

Public Literacy and Community Service

Up until now, the primary focus of this book has been how to participate in public literacy as an individual acting in what you believe to be the public interest. In these last two chapters we will explore opportunites to participate in public literacy in the context of more organized groups: in this chapter, through community service, and in Chapter 10, on the job.

Marian Wright Edelman, founder and president of the Children's Defense Fund, once said that "Service is the rent we pay for living." It's the obligation of everyone, in other words. But community service requires more than just a feeling of "duty"—more, even, than a desire to help. It also calls for reflection on motives, goals, and skills. This chapter will address these issues and explore three kinds of community service you can pursue through public literacy: volunteering, service learning, and grassroots organizing.

Thinking About Service

Community service describes organized, generally uncompensated actions that support or enhance the quality of life in a community. These actions are usually voluntary (an exception is when people are required to perform community service after being convicted of crimes), and most people engage in them because they want to share their talents or resources with others. Community service implies an investment of time and effort rather than simply money or moral support. It often evolves out of the attitude that we are responsible for solving shared problems—even if we're busy and our contributions are modest.

Community service responds to urgent—sometimes life or death—situations. Some urgent problems call for actions that are purely physical, such as building a house or delivering meals to the homebound. Others are rhetorical situations that invite discursive action in the form of public literacy. Identifying the urgent needs of a community includes recognizing problems and determining whether they can best be addressed through community service or some other means.

It is important to think of community service as a relationship as well as a set of actions. It involves you and other members of a community in a partnership that comes at the invitation of the community and that the community believes is important and useful. Developing this kind of relationship requires attention to local knowledge, including local needs and opportunities; a willingness to learn from those we serve, as opposed to a misguided sense of ourselves as "saviors"; and in most cases, a long-term commitment to the issue, the setting, or the people we wish to serve.

Before getting involved in community service, you should honestly evaluate your motives. If they are purely self interested—for example, improving your job prospects, gaining the admiration of others, or fulfilling a requirement for school—you may actually alienate the people whom you are trying to help, creating a negative environment for everyone involved. At the same time, personal interests can be compatible with public interests (see Chapter 1), so if you genuinely want to improve a situation, even in a small way—and even if you expect some personal benefits as well—you might be well suited to this kind of work.

Upon his retirement from the U. S. Supreme Court, Justice Thurgood Marshall remarked, "I did what I could with what I had." This is the essence of community service: figuring out what you like to do and what you do well, then finding or creating opportunities to put those skills to work toward meaningful projects in the public interest.

Volunteering

The most common form of community service is probably *volunteering*: unpaid labor willingly given. You might already have experience with volunteering in the form of tutoring, assisting with political campaigns, working as a museum docent, coaching a youth soccer team, or participating in a clean-up effort. If so, you probably chose to do this work because you had a personal interest in the issue, wanted to get some professional experience, or just thought it would be fun.

If you've never volunteered before, you might legitimately wonder why anyone would bother to work without pay. It's true that volunteering can be mentally and physically exhausting, especially if you are also going to school, working, and caring for a family. But in addition to the satisfaction of knowing that they have contributed to some project in the public interest, most volunteers also report a host of personal benefits from their actions, including feeling more connected to the people around them and becoming more understanding and tolerant of differences. Some actually change the direction of their lives and careers as a result of their efforts, and most feel that they "get back" at least as much as they give.

Public writing is one way to volunteer. Many nonprofit organizations and advocacy groups need people who are confident and versatile writers for public audiences and purposes—people who know how to write effective letters, flyers, grant proposals, and other documents. Such groups often publish their own magazines or newsletters, and may need people who can research and write articles as well.

Most organizations ask potential volunteers to fill out an application before putting them to work. This allows the group to make good use of the applicant's skills while still meeting their own needs. If you are interested in public writing, say so on your application, but don't be discouraged if your supervisors don't immediately put you to work writing petitions. Usually, volunteers start out by learning a variety of duties, skills, and procedures so that they can become more familiar with the mission of the group they're working for. This kind of experience might initially seem unrelated to public writing, but in fact, it's a kind of research: the more you know about the goals and resources of your group, the more effective you can be in recognizing urgent rhetorical situations and responding to them appropriately.

Most communities offer a wide variety of volunteer opportunities so that any potential volunteer can find something of interest. Some communities have agencies that coordinate the volunteer needs of several organizations; if no such agency exists in your community, you can simply call or visit the agency you are interested in working for. Information about volunteering opportunities can usually be found in the phone book, at the Chamber of Commerce or United Way, in local newspapers, and on the Internet. Your campus might also have an office that can direct students to community agencies in need of volunteers.

Service Learning

The goal of *service learning* is to produce civic-minded students who not only think critically about social problems but also take actions to solve them. Toward that end, service learning courses teach academic knowledge and skills in the context of community service projects or some other form of experiential learning. Students earn course credit by applying their learning to some effort in the public interest, usually in collaboration with members of the local community.

Service learning manifests the same ideals of civic education that we considered in Chapter 1. However, it also attempts to intervene in a more recent problem in the United States: indifferent or even hostile relations between universities and their host communities. Since many students (and faculty) are not native to the cities where they attend school, they may see themselves as temporary residents, without any particular investment in the community at large. Service learning assumes that members of a university community are also members of a local community, and thus responsible for its welfare. This includes sharing university resources like libraries, computer facilities, and the expert knowledge and skills that can help solve local problems.

Service learning programs have been developed in many disciplines, including nursing, business, and education. And while these programs often involve professional outreach (e.g., helping residents with their taxes, running a vaccination clinic), they almost always make extensive use of writing, such as creating authentic public documents on behalf of community groups. Students in a communications class, for example, created a Website on behalf of the local Humane Society, as well as a series of flyers that they distributed around campus (fig. 9.1).

In most service learning situations, people are really counting on your writing to assist them in efforts that are important to them and that may directly affect their lives. The "real world" implications of service writing can thus invigorate your academic work with a new sense of purpose, motivate you to do a good job and meet deadlines, and provide you with opportunities to write for audiences other than teachers and peers.

But service learning also poses many potential challenges, which include everything from logistical difficulties (e.g., scheduling conflicts) to inconsistent messages about what constitutes "good writing." As with community service in general, participants in service learning projects must consciously resist the role of "do-gooder." It's fine to feel a sense of pride and satisfaction from your contributions, but if these good feelings create resentment among the people you're assisting, or interfere with the effectiveness of your interaction, then it's time to re-evaluate your motives.

Although it can be difficult to foster relationships in which different constituencies see each other as partners with shared interests, such efforts are supported by several national as well as local public documents. In 1993, for example, President Clinton

PERSONALS

Homeless puppy seeking loving owner. Enjoys playing catch, likes children, and long walks on the beach

Don't let lives end, save a furry friend.

Support the New Hanover Humane Society
call 763-6692 or visit http://humanesociety.wilmington.org
Sponsored by COM 467 Students of UNCW

Figure 9.1. This flyer was created by a group of college students as part of their coursework for a communications class. In addition to helping the students apply their academic learning, the project assisted the local Humane Society in promoting pet adoptions.

signed the National Community Trust Act, which encourages states to develop programs that link schools and communities in joint endeavors to solve social problems. Your campus might have an office that sponsors such endeavors, and individual professors may also develop service learning initiatives.

Grassroots Organizing

Sometimes people have an interest in performing community service but can't find a group whose interests and goals are consistent with their own. Or sometimes an urgent situation arises for which no organized advocacy group yet exists. If you perceive a gap in the community service opportunities at your school or in your community, you might consider organizing a group yourself.

Grassroots organizing describes the efforts on the part of members of everyday and local public spheres to mobilize around some public interest, in effect creating community service opportunities for themselves and likeminded partners. Usually these efforts respond to very specific, very urgent problems, such as the misconduct of an elected official or the threatened demolition of a beloved local landmark. Some grassroots organizations simply disband as these situations are improved or become less urgent, while others continually modify their missions in order to address new problems and concerns.

Local and campus communities are filled with grassroots organizations—some very prominent and well established, others loosely organized and transient. In one small town in North Carolina, for example, citizens formed a group called Concerned Citizens of Southport to oppose the building of a large Wal-Mart store in their community. Although these efforts were ultimately unsuccessful, the group is still active in its community, having expanded its focus to include urban development, taxation, and environmental issues.

The Sweat-Free Campus Campaign began when students realized that their universities were profiting from garment industry sweatshops. Through carefully coordinated publicity campaigns, students have raised awareness about this issue on campuses across the country, persuading officials at several universities to adopt a Code of Conduct that obligates them to take responsibility for the conditions under which their licensed apparel is made. In only two years, the campaign has grown into a national organization, the United Students Against Sweatshops (USAS), with chapters on over 30 campuses.

Grassroots organizations distinguish themselves by starting from scratch: "from the ground up." They represent groups of people working to help themselves and their own communities rather than waiting for someone else to do it.

The student government organization or leadership center on your campus might offer support for grassroots organizing on campus. Another excellent resource is the Center for Campus Organizing, which promotes the creation of alternative newspapers and student-initiated social justice efforts through an extensive Website and a national magazine called *Infusion*. It also publishes a 16-page guide that includes information on how and why to start a grassroots organization, strategies for building membership and a support base, publicity techniques, and event planning. The Center for Campus Organizing can be reached on-line at www.cco.org or at Box 748, Cambridge, MA 02412, (617) 354-9363.

Exercise

Look through your writer's notebook and make a list of interests or concerns that you would like to be more actively involved in. Then look on-line and in local and campus directories for agencies or organizations that might share your interests, or an "umbrella" agency that coordinates volunteer efforts for several groups. Write down their names and contact information, and find out what community service opportunities are available.

Then, find out if there is an office that coordinates service learning efforts at your school. If there is, locate professors who offer service learning courses and ask them about the kinds of projects they have worked on; write down this information in your writer's notebook for future reference. If there isn't an organized service learning program, approach one of your professors to propose a service learning project as part of your semester grade. You might, for example, ask your women's studies professor if you could create a public information kit for the local rape crisis center as your final class project instead of writing a research paper.

CHAPTER 10

Careers in Public Literacy

As this book mentioned earlier, there are many ways to participate in public literacy professionally. Journalism, advertising, public relations, and law are examples of professions whose practitioners create a variety of public documents on a regular basis. In general, though, these professions are limited to people who have college degrees or professional licenses authorizing them to do that work.

There are, however, many other careers that require writing for public audiences and purposes but do not require a particular degree or license. In other words, these careers are available to non-specialists. This chapter introduces you to some of these careers, as well as to people who are involved in them. Many of the people profiled here had no prior experience with public literacy but entered their careers because of their commitment to issues in the public interest. Many of them, moreover, started out as volunteers or interns before becoming full-time employees.

Grant Writer

Patty Chase is the Grants and Budget Director for Friendship Home in Lincoln, Nebraska, a shelter for domestic violence victims and their children. In addition to monitoring her agency's budget, Patty is responsible for preparing all grant proposals that are submitted to various local, state, and national funding sources. As part of her grant writing duties, she researches potential funding sources, meets with staff to understand programmatic needs, and writes all proposals. Patty was a psychology major in college, and since writing papers was a major part of her coursework, she learned the benefits of good research and preparation, being organized and getting things done on time—all of which can mean the difference between a successful and unsuccessful proposal.

Patty's first position at Friendship Home was Children's Program Coordinator, where she was responsible for providing services for the children living at the shelter. Consequently, her first motives for grant writing were, she claims, "strictly personal": finding support to hire an assistant. Buoyed by her successful achievement of this goal, she became "hooked" on writing grants. And although Patty now has several years of grant writing experience, she believes that "there is always room for improvement and modification," and so continues to search for ways to convey information more effectively in the proposals she writes. One important lesson Patty has learned about writing in the public interest is that proposals must explain how the project is going to benefit the women and children served by her agency, not the agency itself.

A typical day for Patty includes writing and conducting research for information she needs to complete her proposals; this might range from finding statistics to calling vendors for price estimates. Patty admits that it can be difficult to make the same information sound compelling, and so it's tempting to get complacent and submit the same proposal over and over again to different funders. Despite these challenges, Patty knows that her work helps to keep women and children safe in times of crisis. She says, "That's what keeps me wanting to learn more about how to be a better grant writer."

Public Information Officer

Mark Boyer is the Public Information Officer for New Hanover County in North Carolina. His job is to publicize, promote a positive public image of, and educate the local public about the functions and services of county government. He accomplishes this by writing news releases, newsletters, brochures, pamphlets, and speeches, and by coordinating special events and participating in video production on behalf of the county government.

Mark sees his role as assisting local media in determining what kind of government information is important to local citizens, including himself: "If I'm interested, then someone else probably is—although maybe not everyone, and not all the time." Because he has to represent the institution of county government as well as its individual members, Mark has had to learn to "speak for" other people, sometimes in their language and style. In order to do this, Mark interviews them to find out what they want to say, then translates their ideas into something the audience will pay attention to.

Mark got into public information after 18 years of news writing at various radio stations around the United States. On the radio you have no photographs or video footage to help people understand your story, he explains, and so you have to do it through words. This experience taught Mark to be concise and concrete, and to edit his writing carefully. Because it's easiest for him to write "for the ear," he has had to learn to be more disciplined about using language "in AP [Associated Press] handbook style" so that he can effectively communicate with members of the media.

Mark believes that it's vital for him to be interested in and conscientious about his work; carelessness not only affects the quality of his writing, but may have negative consequences for the people he serves. Mark respects the time and intelligence of public audiences and so tries to avoid "spin" and instead focus on the bottom line. He describes writing for public audiences and purposes as a continuing educational process—both for himself and his public audiences. Although there's not always a perfect match for how local government works and what the public wants, Mark simply sees this as a challenging fact of his job: "That's fine; that's the democratic process."

Nonprofit Programs Coordinator

Katie Morrow is the program coordinator for the Cape Fear Literacy Council, where she is responsible for almost all the writing that comes out of the organization, including grants, newsletters, appeal letters, reports, general correspondence, and tutor training materials. Currently she is also conducting an informal research project that examines the effect of innovative tutoring methods with learning disabled clients. Previously, Katie has worked as an information officer at Oxfam, a nonprofit international hunger relief organization.

Katie was an art history major in college, but decided not to go into this field after working as a guard at the Hirshhorn Museum in Washington, D.C., one summer. The student workers, all of whom were white, worked alongside full-time security guards, all of whom were black Vietnam veterans. After observing a variety of disparities in their working conditions—including pay scales, office space, and schedules—Katie said, "It was impossible to avoid social justice issues." So she worked as a volunteer after graduating and getting married, and later got a full-time job at Oxfam.

Katie perceives three public spheres in her current position: the donors and potential donors whose names are on their mailing list; newspaper readers and the news media, who spread the word about the Literacy Council's services; and the Council's clients, who are primarily people who don't read or respond to the mail, and require very different types of communication. The complexities of public writing have made Katie keenly interested in readability issues, particularly "how we create a genuine public space for people who are illiterate or semiliterate." Through her work at Oxfam and the Literacy Council, she has become aware that the words she uses and the ways in which she writes determine who will have access to her message.

Because her writing at Oxfam was "internal"—directed toward employees of the organization—Katie describes it as "very safe." The writing she does for the Literacy Council goes to "the outside world," and so she's never sure how, or if, her audience will respond. She admits, though, that "There's a power" to writing that is linked to actions that make a difference in people's lives. This is a lesson her clients are learning, too, as they write short essays for the organization's newsletter, *The Challenger*. Katie finds that as she works with people who are learning to read and write, the motives and agendas they bring to their literacy give her insight into her own work.

Fund Raiser

Barb Weismann is a Development Director for the Seattle Public Theater, where she performs and supervises all tasks related to fund raising. Her responsibilities include writing grant proposals (on average, one a week); writing appeal letters to potential donors; developing themes for fund raising campaigns, and writing the text for brochures and various marketing documents. She also writes thank you letters to grant funders, and corresponds with people requesting information about her organization. Barb wrote her first grants as a volunteer for a homeless shelter, which then hired her to raise money for an elevator renovation.

Barb reports that the most challenging and gratifying aspect of her job is "finding out what works": coming up with new ideas to solve problems and start projects, and figuring out what will give people the incentive to support her organization financially.

Through her experience, Barb has this advice for people interested in public writing. First, learn to edit your own work, and work with others to make suggestions for improvement. (She has actually hired people to do this.) Second, learn what the "formula" writing is in your field, and use it to paint a good "verbal picture" of the problem you're addressing and what you're already doing to help. Don't expect that the old formulas will always work, however, and use your experience and imagination to expand formulas to be successful in new rhetorical situations. Third, don't waste your readers' time with what Barb calls "blah blah blah" writing. Your message must compete with many other messages, so you may only have a few seconds to get readers' attention. And finally, the public is made up of a lot of individuals. Treat them as such.

Citizens Advocate

Alan Harris is an advocate for homeless people in Atlanta, Georgia. Retired from the Social Security Administration since 1988, he began volunteering for soup kitchens in 1983. He now works primarily for the Task Force for the Homeless but describes himself as a "freelancer" who tries to work constructively with the homeless and service providers, wherever the needs are greatest. Alan's work with the homeless combines his lifelong concern about world hunger with his religious faith and commitment to public service. For years he didn't know how to express this concern "and so it lay dormant." But attending an Atlanta-based hunger seminar he decided to "prove his resolve" by getting involved with hunger and homelessness locally.

The most gratifying aspects of Alan's work involve direct human interaction, which he believes is "the best way to find out what's going on." However, he also finds that writing can be a vital means of helping homeless people to meet their basic needs. He has written reports and conducted surveys on the problems facing shelters, and also does extensive writing on behalf of individual clients—assisting them in obtaining birth certificates or corresponding with government agencies, for example.

Alan's most extensive writing project has been to compile a directory of shelters, soup kitchens, and other programs and services designed to assist the local homeless population. He didn't particularly *want* to write this directory, he admits, but was simply responding to an urgent situation: while working at a shelter that was already filled beyond capacity, he didn't know where to send people who needed a place to stay; no centralized resource existed. Alan's work with the Social Security Administration helped him enormously with this project, providing him with the organizational skills to compile and produce the directory and the interpersonal skills to identify the problem and involve as many people as possible in its solution.

Alan knows that the documents he writes have a huge impact on the lives of homeless people, but believes that he could be an even more effective advocate if he had stronger writing skills. And although he describes his work as "a constant stream of gratifying experiences," he especially appreciates the concrete rewards, like helping someone find shelter or shoes that fit, or hearing that a client is doing well in drug treatment. While Alan acknowledges that illiteracy levels are often high among homeless people, he emphasizes that when dealing with disenfranchised groups, information needs to be shared and made accessible in ways that are convenient for the people who need it, not for the agencies that serve them.

Speech Writer

Before returning to graduate school in creative writing, Nancy Jones was Chief Speechwriter for the United States Environmental Protection Agency. In that position, she was responsible for researching and writing speeches for the administrator of the agency, and coordinating with various other offices and officials in the federal government, including the White House. When the administrator was invited to deliver a speech, Nancy gathered a variety of information related to the event, which she translated into a "Speaking Engagement Profile" that she forwarded to the administrator along with his speech (fig. 10.1).

Nancy got into speechwriting through prior work as a newspaper reporter as well as through volunteering for state political campaigns as a college student. This experience helped her to anticipate what questions the press might ask the administrator after his speech, and also taught her how to write under pressure and on very tight deadlines. From writing speeches, Nancy learned how to write in someone else's voice and style—a skill which has helped her in her fiction—and the importance of sometimes suppressing personal opinions when representing the agency and administrator.

Although dealing with the very high level of stress and the frequent crises was one challenging part of her job, Nancy admits that it was also difficult not to receive public credit for her work. The most gratifying part of her work, however, was knowing that her writing and research abilities made a difference in how issues she believed in were received by the public and opinion leaders.

Community Literacy Director

Billie Granger is the Executive Director of the Cape Fear Literacy Council in Wilmington, North Carolina, where she oversees the programmatic and administrative work of the organization, works with the Board of Directors to set policy, corresponds with donors, and participates in tutor training. Although Billie has no college degree, she gained organizational and "people" skills by raising four children, volunteering in her church, and working for 25 years in textile manufacturing. Her first involvement with the Literacy Council was as a volunteer tutor.

Billie believes that one of the most important aspects of her job is "speaking for the silent"—that is, being an advocate for the Literacy Council's clients, many of whom avoid taking part in literacy activities out of shame or embarrassment. She is quick

```
                    SPEAKING ENGAGEMENT PROFILE
                      FOR WILLIAM K. REILLY
                         EPA ADMINISTRATOR

NAME OF GROUP:       Organization for Economic Cooperation and
                     Development (OECD), 24 Environment Ministers

LOCATION:            Paris, France

TIME AND DATE:       10 a.m., January 31, 1991

NUMBER ATTENDING:    Over 200.  Each of the 24 OECD countries is
                     sending a delegation of 5-10 people,
                     including its Environment Minister.  As you
                     know, you are heading the U.S. delegation.

THEME:               Environmental Strategy for the 1990s

OTHER SPEAKERS:      Four or five other Environment Ministers will
                     be speaking on this theme.  Speakers on the
                     first day of the conference will be
                     addressing the themes, "State of the
                     Environment" and "Integration of
                     Environmental and Economic Decision-Making."
                     You will be the first speaker on the second
                     day of the conference, to accommodate your
                     participation in President's State of the
                     Union message.  However, it is appropriate
                     and desirable for you to talk about the
                     issues raised during the first day as well.

INTRODUCING YOU:     You will put up your flag and wait to be
                     recognized.

LENGTH OF SPEECH:    Scheduled for 5 minutes, but 7 to 8 minutes
                     permissible.

ROOM SETTING:        Large, square table.  Two delegates per
                     country sit around the square. Other
                     delegates sit behind in rows that run six
                     deep behind each side of the square.  You
                     will speak from your position at the table.

PRESS:               No press during session.  Press briefing
                     scheduled for late afternoon of January 31.
                     Speakers are invited to release longer
                     versions of their remarks to the press.  A
                     USIS wire story is being prepared based on
                     your written remarks.

OTHER:               EPA is urging OECD to initiate annual
                     environmental policy reviews for its 24
                     member countries to assure consistency and
                     coordination.
```

Figure 10.1. The categories of this Speaking Engagement Profile resemble the categories of the rhetorical situation: urgency, audience, and constraints.

to admit that she herself is "more a talker than a writer," and it is only through exposure to different audiences and genres at work that she has learned to write more formally. Billie's openness with her own continuing process of literacy learning gives her credibility with her clients, all of whom are adults struggling with reading and writing.

The Literacy Council has to be visible within the community in order to reach the people who need its services; furthermore, it must maintain a good rapport with the county government, large granting institutions, and individual donors who support it financially. The responsibility for cultivating these relationships often rests with Billie, who says that when you are representing the organization, you can't always speak your mind. "The public is people," she observes, and you have to know who you're communicating with in order to be effective.

Community Activists

Mark Rauscher and Billy Barwick are Co-Chairs of the Wilmington, North Carolina Chapter of the Surfrider Foundation, an international organization dedicated to beach conservation. The acronym guiding the Surfrider mission is "CARE": conservation, activism, research, and education. Members fulfill this mission by doing presentations at schools, setting up information booths at local fairs and festivals, sponsoring beach clean-ups, and lobbying for environmentally friendly legislation. Mark is also a graduate student in coastal geology, and frequently presents his research findings at Surfrider meetings.

Because Mark has access to email and the Internet, he is responsible for much of the writing and correspondence for the local Surfrider chapter. The national organization sponsors an e-mail listserv for local chapters to discuss issues, ask questions, or solicit ideas from other members. Mark monitors these discussions and forwards relevant information to local Surfriders. He also writes articles describing chapter activities for Surfrider's newsletter, *Making Waves*, maintains the local chapter's Website, and writes letters and press releases. Mark solicits feedback and approval from other members before publishing any writing on behalf of the organization.

Since they interact with government agencies such as the Department of Natural Resources, Billy and Mark have access to information that doesn't necessarily make it onto the news. They bring this information to other members and use it to formulate activist agendas. In addition to "phone-ins," where Surfrider members call politicians and encourage them to support environmentally friendly legislation, Billy and Mark have also organized letter writing parties, at which they provide newspaper clippings related to coastal issues and sample letters of concern that members can consult in order to communicate effectively with local, state, and national politicians.

Billy and Mark got involved in Surfrider because of their mutual love of surfing and the coast, but both admit that activism can be draining: it's difficult to keep up with the paperwork and efforts often fail. Billy remains active in the organization because it allows him to channel his frustration with beach degradation in positive ways. Mark—who jokingly describes himself as a "full-time surfer, part-time worker"—says he wants to be able to not just study the coast, but do something to preserve it. "I love the coast and I'm totally saturated in it," says Mark. "It's all that I do." Although Mark and Billy are gratified by such large-scale victories as influencing national legislation, they also cite the importance of smaller successes, like when someone thanks them for making the beach a place that everyone can enjoy.

Conclusions

Clearly, there are many overlaps in these job descriptions: people who write grants might need to prepare reports or train volunteers; people who work in politics might find themselves raising money or writing press releases as well as "cleaning toilets," as Billie Granger put it. One reason for this is that jobs that serve public interests are often located in the nonprofit sector, where erratic budgets and large volunteer staffs necessitate more flexible roles and organizational structures.

The careers described here represent only a few of those available to people who want to incorporate public literacy into their professional as well as their personal lives. The important thing to remember is that any issue can be a public issue, and any career can inspire public writing. With your eyes and ears open and your notebook handy, you can write your way into public life, and shape the public issues of the next millennium.

Exercise

Locate a person in your community whose job involves public writing; it need not be someone who works in a position described here. Then, arrange to interview them about the kind of writing they do. The profiles for this chapter were based on the following questionnaire, which you may wish to adapt:

Name:

Job Title:

Employer:

1. Please describe your job. What are your primary responsibilities? What kinds of writing do you do?

2. What personal, educational, work, and/or volunteer experiences prepared you for this job?

3. What have you learned about writing from your job? What have you learned about working with the public?

4. What are the most challenging parts of your job? What are the most gratifying?